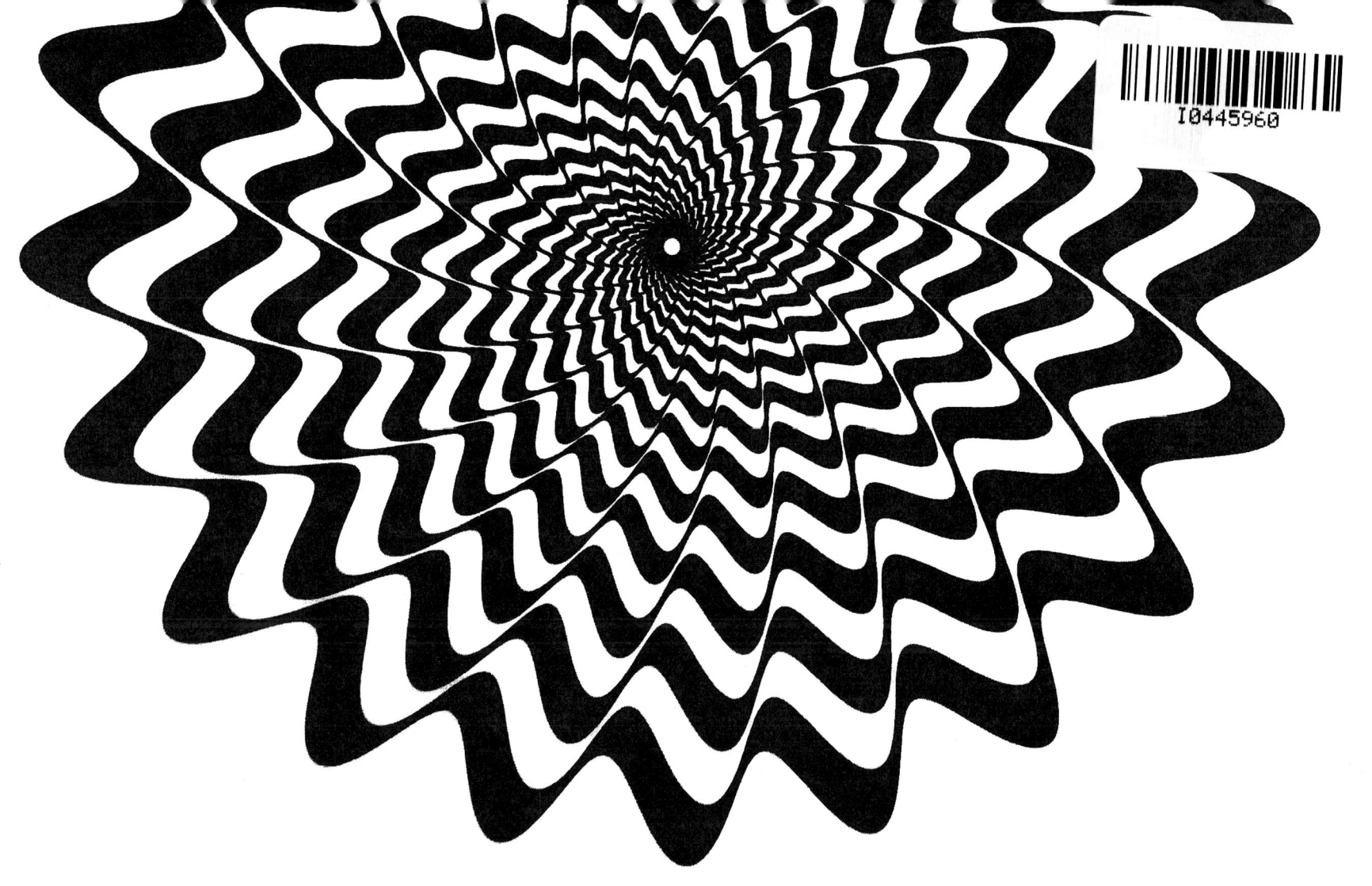

CYBERNETHISMS

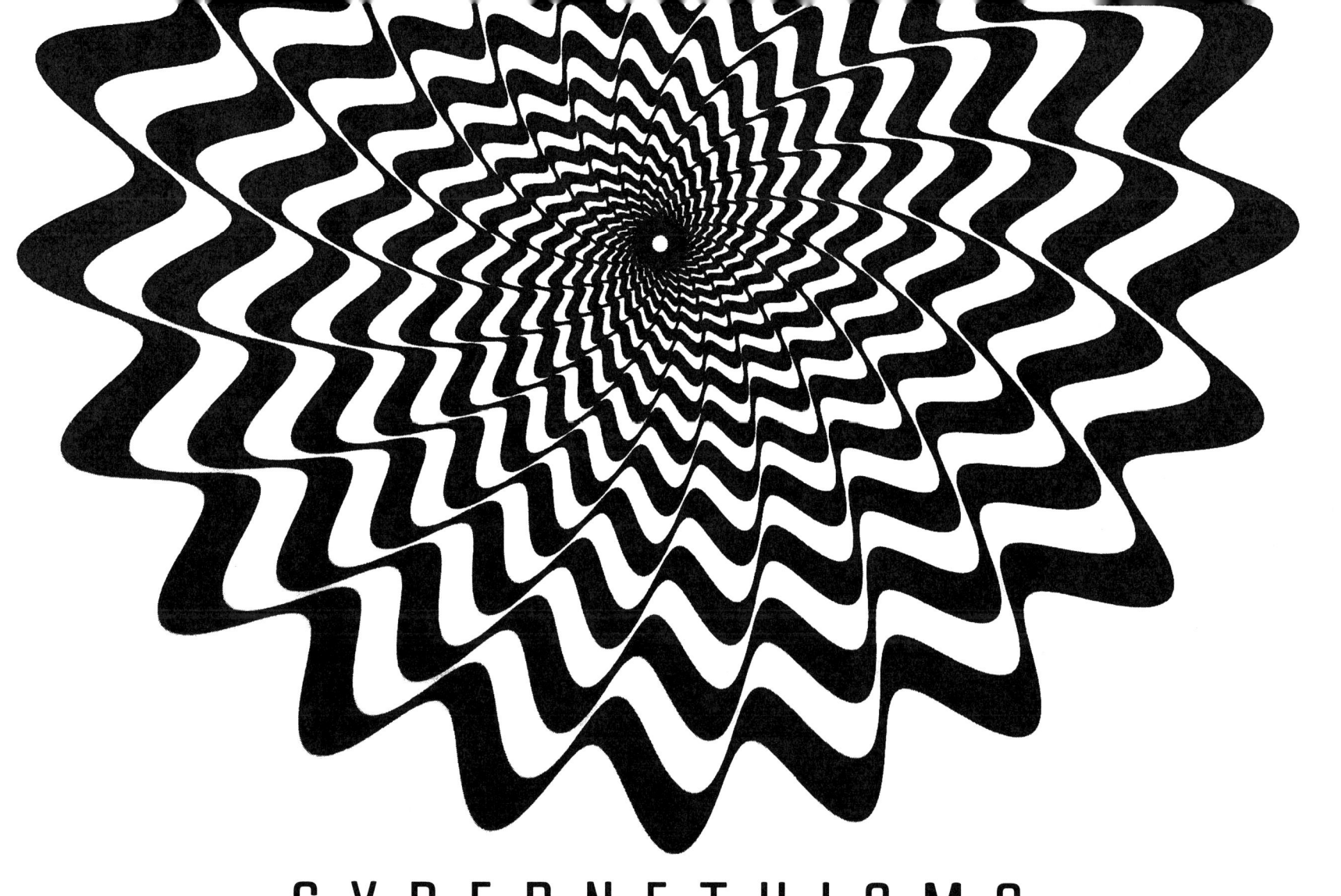

CYBERNETHISMS
ALDO GIORGINI'S COMPUTER ART LEGACY

ESTEBAN GARCÍA BRAVO

PURDUE UNIVERSITY PRESS | WEST LAFAYETTE, INDIANA

Cataloging-in-Publication data on file at the Library of Congress.

All images are © Aldo Giorgini, Purdue University Virginia Kelly Karnes Archives and Special Collections, unless noted Δ.
Δ Aldo Giorgini's estate, Lafayette, Indiana.

TO ALDO

CONTENTS

ACKNOWLEDGMENTS

When I became interested in the potential artistic possibilities of computer code, my wife, Stephanie, was the first to see the potential academic research in my new area of interest. Thank you, Stephanie, for your companionship and support throughout this entire process, and for the many hours devoted to proofreading my first pseudo-English scribbles.

During my first visit to the computer graphics department at Purdue University, I was welcomed by Drs. La Verne Harris, James Mohler, and Craig Miller. These professors consistently guided, encouraged, and supported my research throughout my doctoral studies, and I am extremely grateful for their caring advice and mentoring during this adventure. I also would like to thank Dr. Patrick Connolly for his valuable feedback on this research and for his leadership in the department. All of these individuals have been strong advocates of my work, and I would like to express my endless gratitude for their support.

Of course, this research would have not been possible without the help of the Giorgini family: Flaviano Giorgini, Massimiliano Giorgini, and Kelly Paez-Urbano. Thank you, Flaviano and Massimiliano, for granting me access to your father's materials. I truly appreciate the trust you placed in me to allow me to explore his studio. Additionally, special thanks to Massimiliano for devoting so many hours of your time to answer my many questions about your father. I also would like to thank Kelly for so graciously permitting me inside the Giorgini residence to perform this investigation.

Special thanks to Dr. Elizabeth Mix, who helped me shape the thematic structure of this study and who patiently reviewed the first drafts of this biography. Lastly, I would like to thank Nisha Nagarajan for assisting in the final formatting of this book, serving as an assistant editor, and helping with the review, references, and appendices of this book.

INTRODUCTION

I still remember my first time using a computer. The year was 1988. I was in first grade, and as I watched my brother plug a beige-colored keyboard into our television, my excitement grew for my first opportunity to experience the Commodore VIC-20, an amazing visual playground. The programs were stored in the form of a cassette tape and loaded into the computer by typing commands from the keyboard. One of the features I especially loved was the ability to create color pictures in the 22-by-23 pixel grid of VIC-20's screen.

I was artistically inclined from a very early age. My school also had lots of VIC-20s, and our computing class taught us a language called LOGO. In LOGO, the user typed a list of commands to depict shapes on the screen. We would have assignments in which we had to "draw" various images, such as an ice cream cone or a hexagon. Simple commands—such as RT 90, for rotating the line 90 degrees, or functions like REPEAT—were my first exposure to the elements of programming.

As time passed, I witnessed fast development of graphics. As I matured, so did the technology, including computer games, interactive CD-ROMs, scanners, and the Internet. Gradually, images became more colorful and realistic; the new computer interfaces started looking like desktops or artist's studios with "tools" for painting digital "canvases."

I came to Purdue University from Colombia in 2005 to study for an MFA in electronic and time-based media. It was a unique experience to experiment with all that technology had to offer to the fine arts; we had classes on robotics, interfaces, programming languages, and digital imaging.

I became familiar with the work of Aldo Giorgini within my first months in Indiana. I was introduced to Massimiliano, Giorgini's son, at a party at my brother's apartment. During our first conversation, Massimiliano told me all about his father's pioneering work in computer art. I learned that much of his father's original artwork and papers were still in Lafayette. Massimiliano and his wife, Kelly, lived at the Giorgini residence, where Giorgini's studio remained, nearly untouched since his death in 1994. I was a computer artist myself and was very excited to learn that my new place of residence had its own computer art history—to my surprise, a history that had not yet been written.

When I got home, I did a quick image search on Aldo Giorgini. The piece called *I Ain't a Spiral* (Figure 1) was on my screen within minutes. The work was mysterious on many levels. Formally, the composition showed an algorithmic design of black and white ripples that drew me to an optical effect that was both dazzling and pleasant. Aside from the visual aspects, however, the date of the image called my attention—1974 seemed like an early date for a computer-based work.

It was those mysteries within his work that compelled and inspired me to do this research and to understand Giorgini's developments in computer art. When I made my first visit to Giorgini's former studio in the basement of the house on Berkley Road, I could almost believe that Giorgini was still alive. The amount of files, folders, and artwork lying around were reminiscent of an artist working on a big project. After that, I visited the Giorgini residence more and more regularly, and I became familiar with Giorgini's intricate methods. In an archaeological way, documents, paintings, and computer codes resurfaced, as I scavenged through every container and cabinet of his studio. Every time I found a new image hiding inside an envelope or a cardboard box, I became

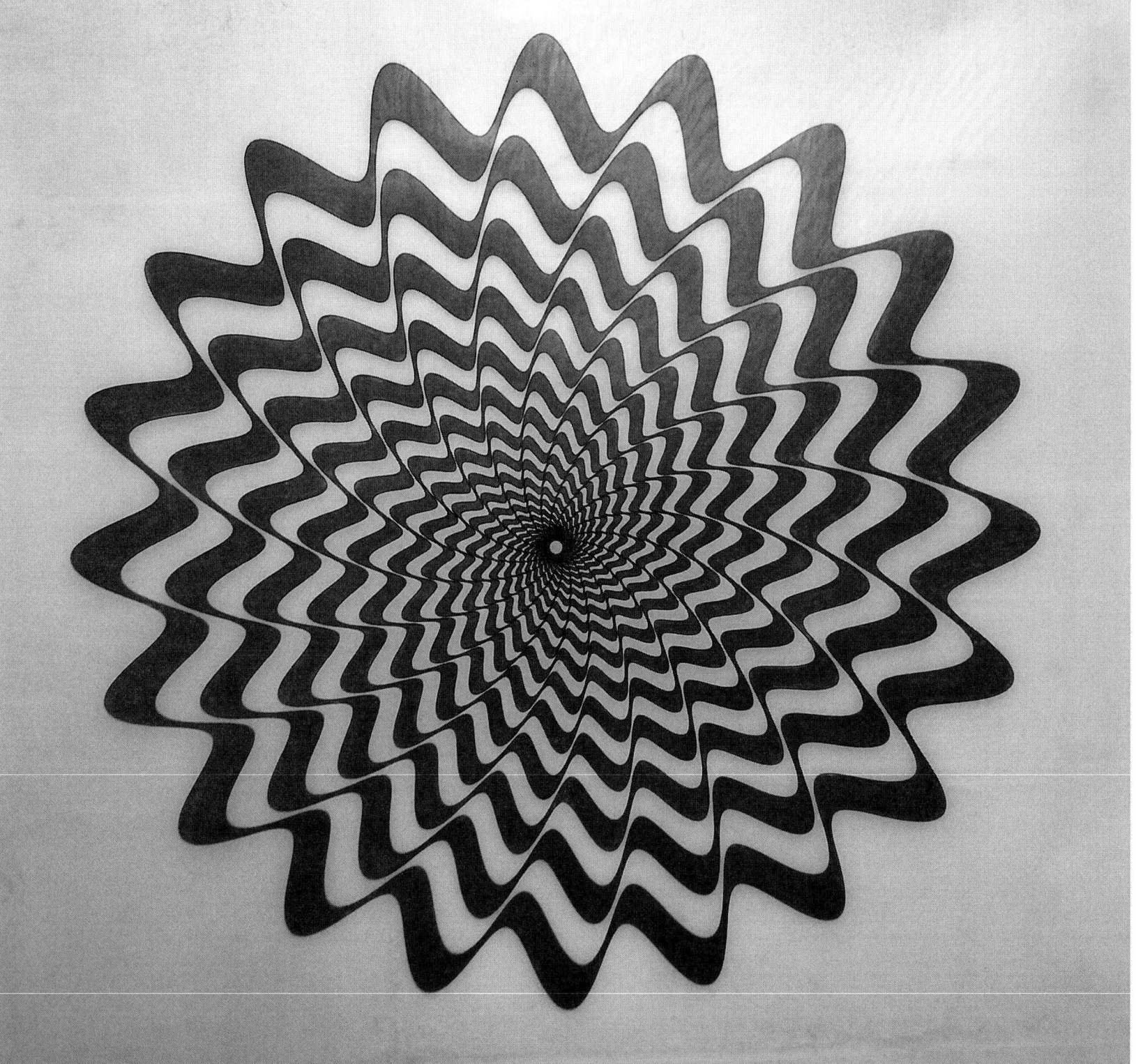

increasingly intrigued with his process. This book is the result of an exhaustive four-year inspection of Giorgini's studio, the place where he produced his computer art. I was able to create a narrative, my interpretation of who Aldo Giorgini was; however, though my investigation was thorough, it would be impossible to recreate a true representation of Giorgini's persona. For this reason, the final section of this book is devoted to a selection of Giorgini's unpublished manuscripts. These documents reveal his unique philosophy toward art and computers.

Giorgini worked extensively developing algorithms for graphics, but he also theorized about the meanings of a then new computer-aided art practice. The year 1973 marked Giorgini's deliberate decision to start making art with computers. In that year, he titled his first computer art series *Cybernethisms*, a word that inspired the title of this book. The word is derived from *cybernetics*, a term coined by Norman Wiener in 1948, which describes the scientific study of control and communication with machines.[1] In its origins, the interchangeable terms *cybernetic art* and *computer art* were used by pioneering artists to describe their process. The translated use of the term, *arte cibernético*, also was common among computer artists in Spanish-speaking countries, such as Manuel Barbadillo or José María Yturralde, who started their computer-based practice in the spring of 1968 at the Centro de Cálculo at the University of Madrid.[2] Giorgini was aware of both associations of cybernetics: first, for the use of computer code and logic as a form of communication with the machine; and second, because of its association with an international art movement. In the chapter "Computer Art in Context," I focus on providing a historic background to contextualize Giorgini within a larger group of artists from his generation.

Although Giorgini's art is known among a select group of computer artists and theorists, his contribution has been relatively unknown, possibly because of his premature death in 1994. However, Giorgini's ideas have resonated in the minds of influential individuals such as the computational theorist Raymond Kurzweil. In *The Age of Intelligent Machines*, a seminal book in the realm of cybernetics and artificial intelligence, Kurzweil references Giorgini's art an example of how some forms may only be possible to create through computational methods.[3] Giorgini's work also was appealing to a community of computer artists who recall his compositions as "striking"[4] or just "better," as Charles Csuri mentioned in personal correspondence:

> Aldo Giorgini is an important artist in the early history of computer art, in fact, a better artist than many who have received more media attention. [. . .] But the reason I like his work better has little to do with the code or the procedures. It's the aspect which transcends the code and makes it art which cannot be described in logical terms.[5]

Like Giorgini, many early computer artists also were outside the scope of historians until recently. Margit Rosen, a researcher in the history of computer art, explains that many of the earliest prints were forgotten "behind closets" until a recent historian's renewed interest on this era.[6] As part of an ongoing discussion, this book will bring to the table questions on whether early computer artifacts should be preserved or not, due to the disembodied nature of code-based art practices. What constitutes the artwork in pieces that are mediated by a computer? This long-standing question (that is inherent to the medium) contrasts with the historical value of some of the resulting artifacts produced by computers during the past fifty or even sixty years.

Lately the topic of preservation of digital and pre-digital[7] art has inspired new books, research, and forums. Some artists, curators, collectors,

Figure 1. *I Ain't a Spiral*, 1973. Acrylic paint on Mylar, 36 x 36 in.

and archivists have discussed strategies of preservation of digital memory extensively. Frieder Nake, one of the first artists in the world who exhibited computer art, recently explained on an Internet message board[8] that most of the early works of computer art were based entirely on a paper medium, but simply because of the specific nature of the computing technologies that were available at that time. Various institutions recently have focused on developing mechanisms to catalog and preserve early computer art; two of the most known are the collection at the Victoria and Albert Museum and the Charles A. Csuri Project at the Ohio State University.

Inspired by these two initiatives, I sought to pursue a similar project on a much smaller scale. Broadly speaking, my task consisted of both unveiling and understanding Giorgini. I approached the subject with a practical framework in mind, focusing on the study of the physical outputs and artifacts that resulted from his process. I soon realized the importance of these materials and contacted the Purdue University Virginia Kelly Karnes Archives and Special Collections Research Center for help in the task of preserving these resources. In the section titled "Future of the Collection," I elaborate on the process of research, documentation, and preservation for this particular case study.

Giorgini's untouched studio provided a window through time that allowed me to look into the context in which the works were created. This glimpse of his life offered a larger view of a seminal moment for computer-based art practices—a vibrant scene of artists and scientists who struggled to get their new interdisciplinary ideas accepted or even acknowledged by other art critics or academics. This book also contrasts Giorgini's participation in the computer art movement with some of the technological advances in digital imaging that occurred throughout the 1970s and early 1980s.

The aim of this biography was to explain the technologically based art of Giorgini, while inspecting relevant experiences during his lifetime. This book explores Giorgini's simultaneous development as an artist and scientist, and describes his professional progression, from his early years in Eritrea to his days as a professor of civil engineering at Purdue University. Giorgini became familiar with the computer in 1968, when he produced his first computer visualizations of meteorological data, when graphics technologies were incipient. Later, he began creating programs to visualize other phenomena in the physical world: a fluid interrupted by a cylinder or the effects of light over surfaces. His highly mathematical models allowed him to create complexly beautiful and almost natural shapes. The computer programs were both platforms for making art and artworks themselves, introducing coding as a new creative practice. Giorgini's computer art images received significant acclaim during the 1970s, and his scientific images received similar attention in the 1980s. Giorgini could have been just an artist or just a scientist, but in practice, he pursued both simultaneously. His artistic explorations on computational forms provided him with a groundwork in which to create realistic simulations to be applied in the sciences. Using an eclectic studio practice that combined different tools and processes, Giorgini became an accomplished artist. The over three hundred original art pieces[9] and documentation that now remain at the Purdue University Archives and Special Collections are testimonials of this legacy.

My intent is to contribute to the creation of new histories from a generation of artists that seemed to have been practically ignored. While completing this study, my research raised a renewed interest in Giorgini's work among a community of electronic artists and researchers. Portions of this book have been featured in academic journals and conferences of electronic art and computer art history. Examples include *Leonardo: Journal of the International Society for the Arts, Sciences and Technology*; SIGGRAPH 2011;[10] ISEA 2013;[11] and Media Art Histories 2013: RENEW.[12]

Learning about Giorgini's life and his unique practice was a thrilling experience that I would like to share with readers. I hope that you enjoy it as much as I did. Today, Giorgini continues to inspire me to pursue the path that he and his colleagues began.

Notes

1. Norbert Wiener, *Cybernetics: Or the Control and Communication in the Animal and the Machine* (Cambridge, MA: MIT Press, 1948).

2. Enrique Castaños-Ales, "Los Orígenes del Arte Cibernético en España," 2000, http://www.enriquecastanos.com/tesisindice.htm.

3. Raymond Kurzweil, *The Age of Intelligent Machines* (Cambridge, MA: MIT Press, 1990), 514.

4. Colette Bangert, interview by author, September 4, 2011.

5. Charles Csuri, personal communication with author, August 25, 2011.

6. Margit Rosen, ed., *A Little-Known Story About a Movement, a Magazine, and the Computer's Arrival in Art: New Tendencies and Bit International, 1961–1973* (Cambridge, MA: MIT Press, 2011), 10.

7. *Pre-digital* is used here to refer to works that were mediated by the computer before the term *digital* became popular.

8. Frieder Nake, "[Yasmin_discussions] Fwd: FW: Keeping works," *Yasmin List,* June 30, 2014, http://yasminlist.blogspot.com/2014/06/yasmindiscussions-fwd-fw-keeping-works.html.

9. At the Giorgini residence, more than a thousand originals were found; however, many of them were either exact painted replicas or physically damaged.

10. Esteban Garcia and David Whittinghill, "Art and Code: The Aesthetic Legacy of Aldo Giorgini," *Leonardo: Journal of the International Society for the Arts, Sciences and Technology* 44, no. 4 (2011): 309–16.

11. Esteban Garcia, "Stretch: An Early Software Art Framework by Aldo Giorgini," Paper presented at the 19th International Symposium of Electronic Arts, Sydney, Australia, June 2013, http://www.isea2013.org/events/digital-experimental-arts/.

12. Esteban Garcia, "Photo and Palette: Early Pixel-Based Computer Art," Paper presented at the Media Art Histories 2013: RENEW, the 5th International Conference on the Histories of Media Art, Science, and Technology, Riga, Latvia, October 8–11, 2013.

I. A BIOGRAPHY OF ALDO GIORGINI

THE BEGINNINGS

In the spring of 1934 in Voghera, Italy, Aldo Pasquale Giuseppe Giorgini was born to parents Adelmo and Pierina. At this time in Italy, under the dictatorship of Mussolini, working-class families were encouraged to relocate to Africa through monetary rewards and tax incentives in an effort to expand the Italian empire for colonization efforts. So when Giorgini was three years old, his family moved to Decamere, in the country of Eritrea (former Ethiopia). During World War II, Decamere was reclaimed by the allied forces. Some Italians, included Giorgini, remained in Eritrea as war refugees. He befriended an Italian painter and sculptor named Carlo Ingegneri, who also was a refugee in Eritrea. From age ten to fifteen, Giorgini became Ingegneri's apprentice, mixing pigments and combining colors for Carlo's paintings.[1] Ingegneri was a long-lasting influence on Giorgini, who would later choose to become an artist himself, implementing some of the same color mixing and texturing techniques at a later stage in his life. Figure 2 shows the young Giorgini posing with his dog, Blacky, in Decamere, Eritrea, on December 16, 1946.

Upon his return to Voghera at age fifteen, Giorgini met Ambrogio Casati, an artist who was part of the Italian Futurist movement. Casati took on Giorgini as an apprentice, and for three years they worked together to restore old masters' frescoes and oil paintings that had been damaged during World War II. This apprenticeship provided him with experience that would serve as a solid groundwork for painting.

At age eighteen, Giorgini received a full scholarship to the University of Pavia, where he finished his undergraduate studies in engineering. Afterward, he commenced work on a doctorate in mechanical engineering,[2] which he completed in 1959. He then became an associate professor of hydraulics at the Polytechnic University of Torino from 1959 until 1961. In 1964, Aldo married Elena (Figure 3), the love of his life,[3] whom he had met while working as a professor at the University of Torino. After Giorgini was awarded a Fulbright grant as an exchange scholar to Colorado State University in 1966, the newlyweds settled in Fort Collins, where Giorgini would complete a doctorate in civil engineering.

Between 1966 and 1967, Giorgini worked as a postdoctoral fellow at the National Center for Atmospheric Research in Boulder, Colorado. It was here that he produced his first computer-aided visualizations. During this period, he started exploring computing to create visual forms. Giorgini created dynamic images that could be manipulated with variable numerical parameters. Through mathematical models, Giorgini was able to render image sequences of physical phenomena, such as water turbulences. He computed his calculations and visualized them as printed plots of paper with images and printed text

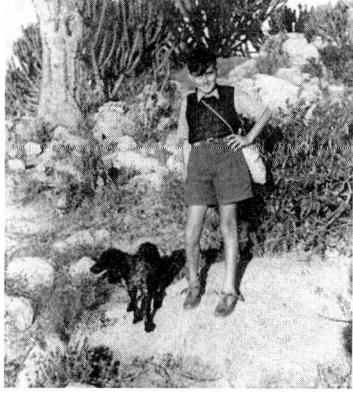

Figure 2. Aldo Giorgini in Decamere at age twelve. Δ Photograph courtesy of Aldo Giorgini's estate.

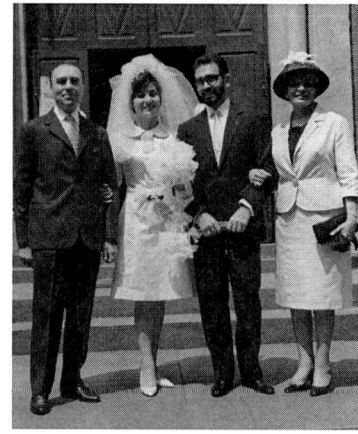

Figure 3. Aldo and Elena at their wedding in 1964. Δ Photograph courtesy of Aldo Giorgini's estate.

with variable numbers. For example, many images were in the function of a variable T, for time, given in seconds. Giorgini was able to visualize the different stages of a simulated turbulence, with vortices and swirls that later inspired his artistic themes.

In 1967 he moved to West Lafayette, Indiana, to work as an assistant professor in the School of Civil Engineering at Purdue University. While there, he completed another doctorate in physics. In the summer of 1969 and 1970, Giorgini returned to the National Center for Atmospheric Research as a visiting scientist. Around this time, Elena gave birth to their first two sons, Massimiliano and Flaviano, who were born in 1968 and 1970, respectively.[4]

By 1971, Giorgini had produced some of his first CalComp visualizations that simulated turbulence and other hydraulic phenomena. At Purdue's School of Civil Engineering, Giorgini experimented with software production and pen plotter printers. The resulting images resembled the flow of fluids through geometrical descriptions, such as cylinders and points. The turbulence visualization took into consideration stochastic models to include an element of chance in the representation. Giorgini quickly became an expert in probabilistic methods that allowed him to almost accurately simulate and represent the behavior and the movement of large masses of fluid variations in time.

Early Works

While developing computer visualizations, Giorgini decided to perfect his artistic practice as a painter. In 1972, he collaborated with Purdue student Dan Cook on a series of small-format paintings. Giorgini and Cook called the series *Chastiques*; they consist of about two hundred paintings of abstract and colorful forms. A liquid style was achieved by mixing oil- and water-based paints and transferring them onto canvas paper. The *Chastiques* were a means by which to visualize fluid dynamics. By combining different enamels and acrylics, Giorgini and Cook created images that looked like organic color splashes. An example of a *Chastique* can be seen in Figure 4.

Another painting collaboration with Cook was a mural entitled *Hymn to Achievement*, which was originally on display at the civil engineering building at Purdue from 1972 until 2012. This 24-foot-by-7-foot triptych depicts a war scene represented with the dark image of a soldier next to a cow skull, with an atomic bomb in the background. The painting also depicts abstract designs that recall scientific representations, such as molecular structures, crystals, and spaceships. Giorgini's intent was to make a statement about how technological and scientific advancements should not be at the service of warfare.

Technological Art

In 1973, Giorgini began his first artistic experimentation with computers. His research, particularly in hydraulics visualization while at Purdue, greatly influenced the aesthetics of his work. Giorgini explained, "I started 'playing around' with some of the computer drawings that were made as illustration of the research done. From here to the purposeful use of the computer as an art tool the pace was very short."[5]

In the spring of 1973, Giorgini created a poster for Eugene Cernan's presentation at Purdue, entitled "Technology and Man's Future." Cernan was a Purdue alumnus who had recently walked on the moon in 1972 as commander of the last lunar mission Apollo 17. The poster, seen in Figure 5, shows a handmade design with an interlocking arrow and question mark. As a background for the design, Giorgini deliberately chose to use a computer-generated pattern that he had created in 1971 with J. R. Travis for a scientific image in a report entitled *Numerical Simulation of the Navier-Stokes Equations in Fourier Space*.[6] This poster marks the beginning of Giorgini's computer art practice, combining both handmade and technological elements.

Figure 4. An example of *Chastique* from 1972. Oil and acrylic on canvas paper.

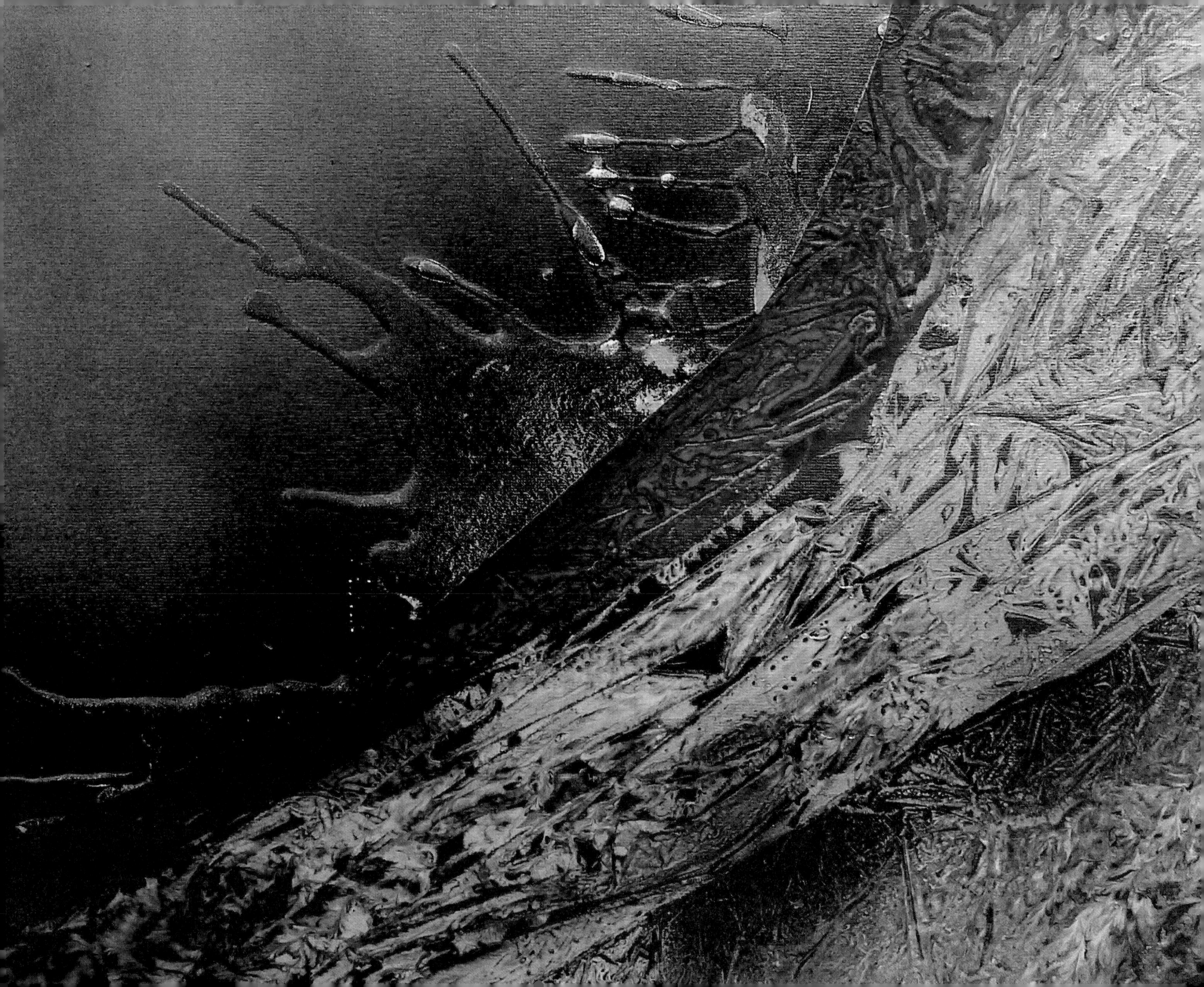

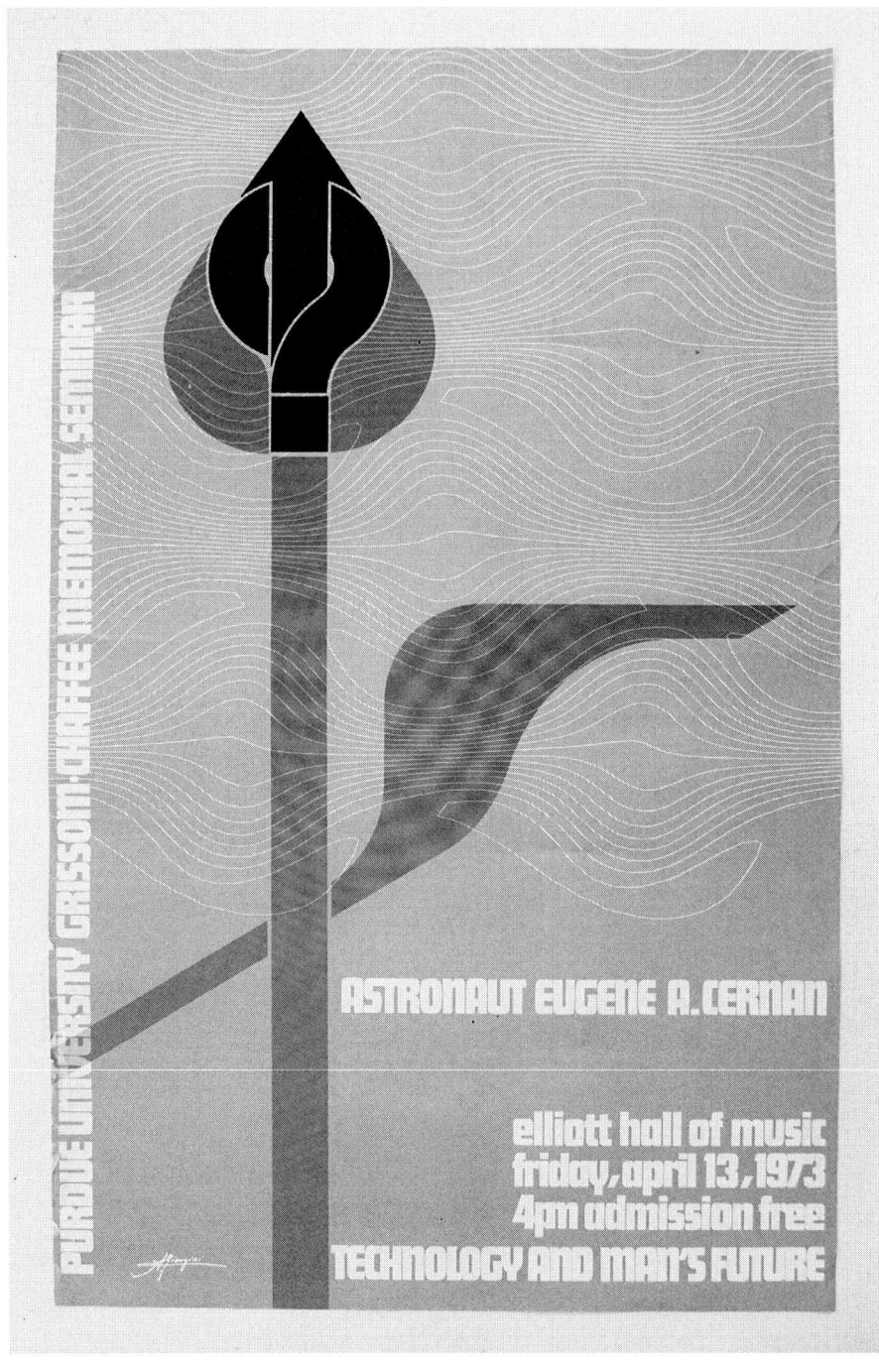

Figure 5. Poster featuring computer-aided designs from 1973.

Shortly after Cernan's visit, Giorgini created his first computer art images: *Don't Go Bananas* (Figure 6); *Cybernethism* (Figure 7); *Arthropodics* (Figure 8); and *I Ain't a Spiral* (see Figure 1 on page x). *Don't Go Bananas* consists of the pattern from Cernan's poster combined with multiple copies of the same image. In work such as *Cybernethism* and *Arthropodics*, it is apparent that Giorgini used multiple copies of his paintings to create new designs by overlapping the rippled motifs in different directions. Giorgini's first computer-aided works were timidly painted black at occasional intersecting spots. As he became more comfortable with the technique, he decided to paint all the intersecting shapes, which produced a full pattern. Figure 8 shows *Arthropodics*, with an incomplete pattern.

The advanced printing technologies Giorgini had available to him at Purdue played a big part in his experimentation. His lab included a CalComp pen plotter, an instrument that draws lines on paper at the execution of computer code. Giorgini envisioned the creative potential of CalComp as a medium for art production. His mathematical formulas were transferred to machine logic using computer code in order to create visual outputs. Giorgini used an early version of the language Fortran and loaded it in the CalComp 563 plotter. The plotter was loaded with bond paper rolls and drew the contour lines in black ink. Purdue's resources allowed Giorgini's visual research to develop quickly as he could plot on a daily basis.

Giorgini's studio in the basement of his residence held thousands of CalComp prints revealing his complete artistic process. Once a design had been plotted on paper, he began an elaborate handmade process and complemented the computer work with paint. In a 1975 research report he wrote with Wei-Chung Chen, entitled "Interfaces," Giorgini explains, "In the case where the output needs further intervention by the artist in order to produce the final art piece, the term of computer-aided art will apply."[7]

This chronological description of Giorgini's early life show the experiences and research that laid the foundations of his career as a computer artist.

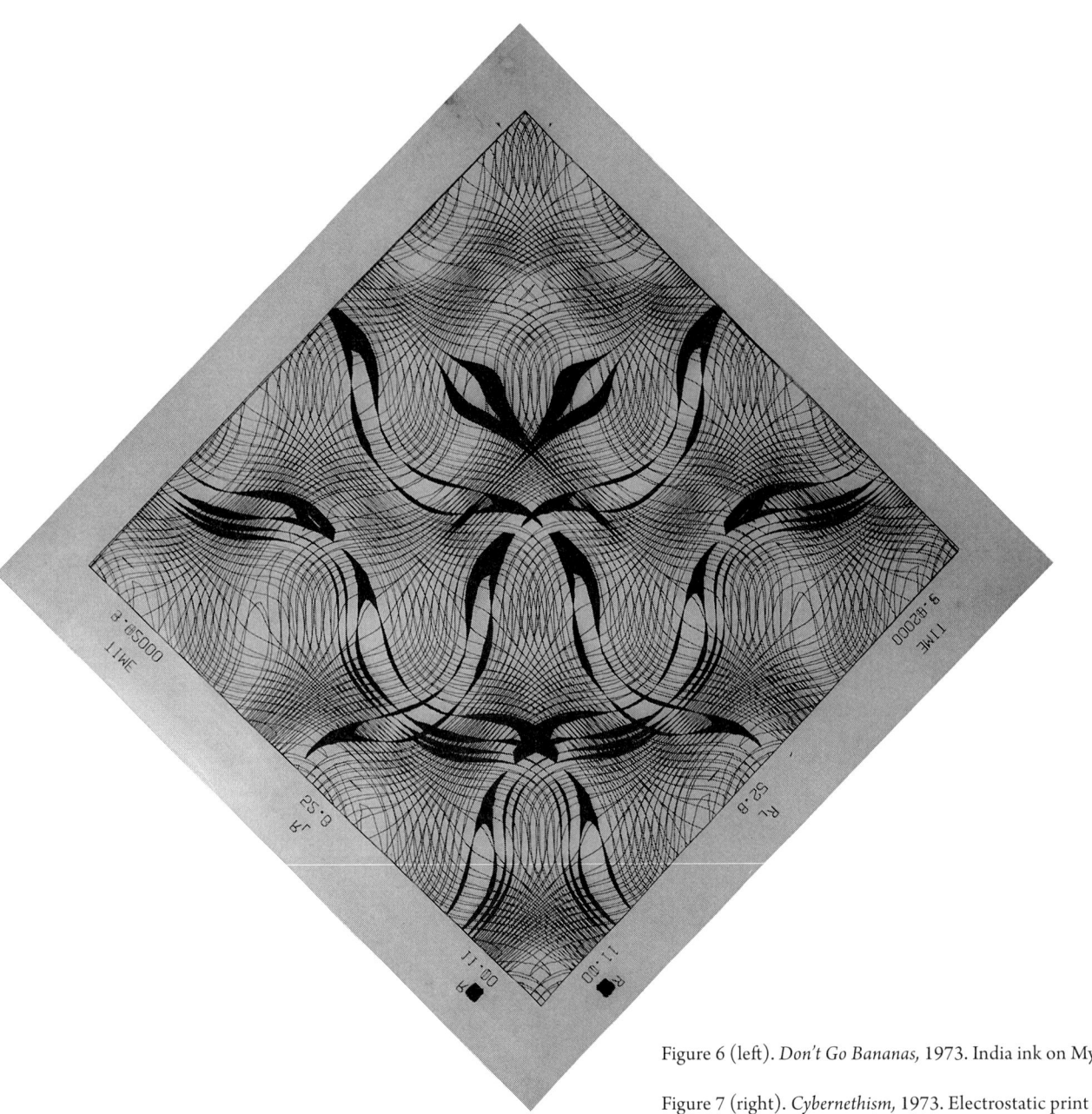

Figure 6 (left). *Don't Go Bananas,* 1973. India ink on Mylar, 36 x 36 in.

Figure 7 (right). *Cybernethism,* 1973. Electrostatic print on Mylar, 36 x 36 in.

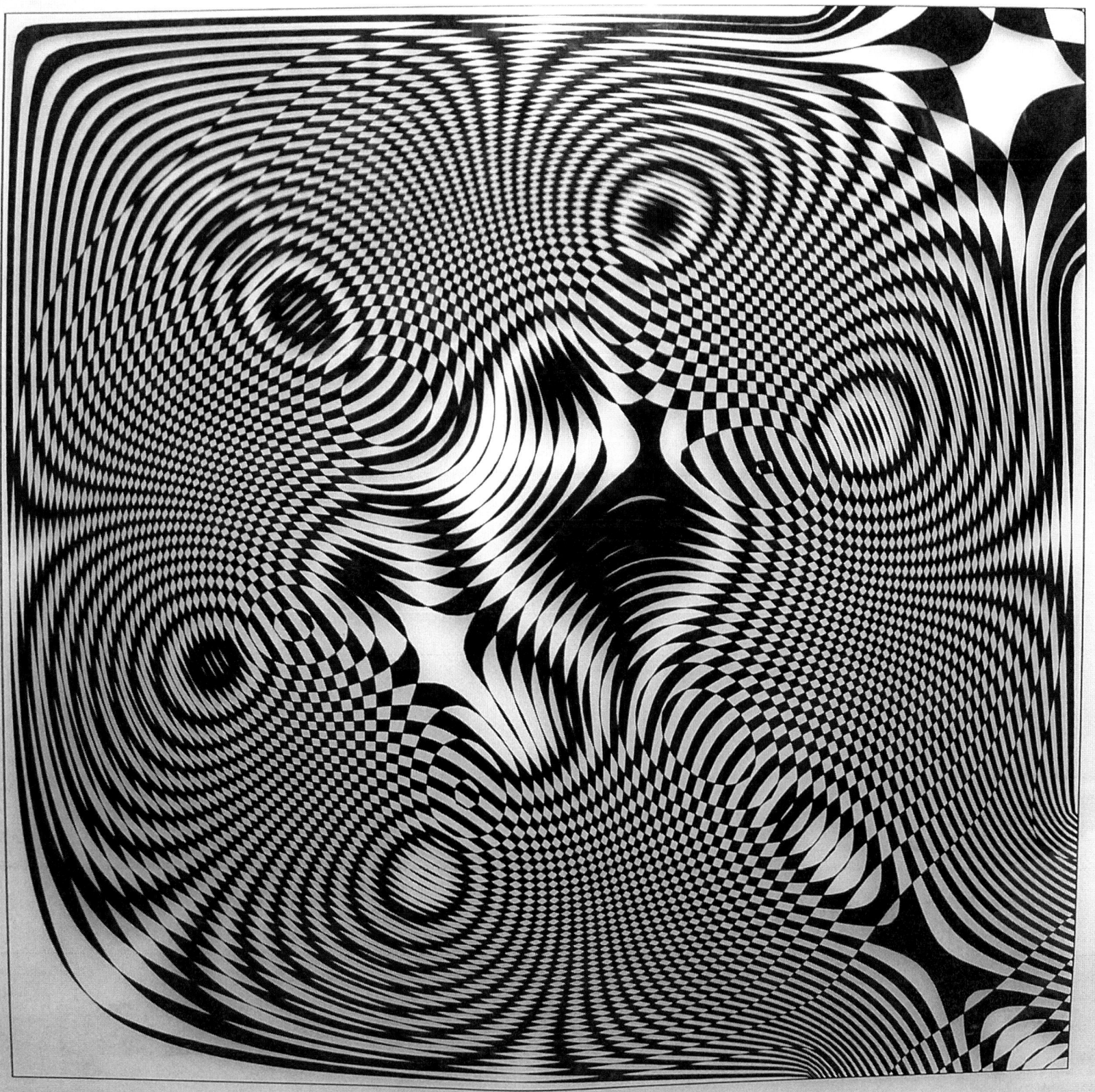

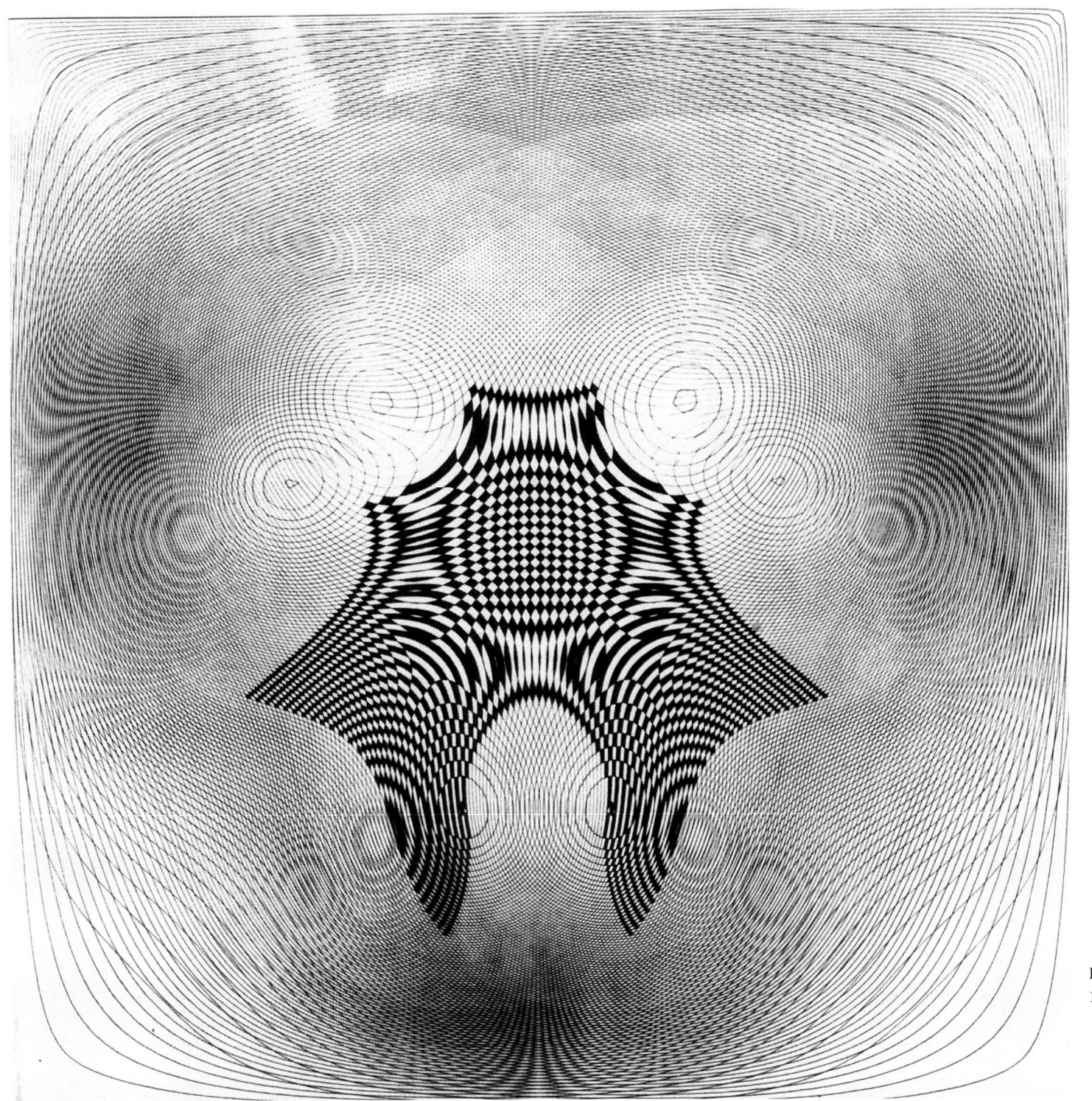

Figure 8. *Arthropodics,*
1973. Photograph.

FIELDS: A NUMERICAL VISUAL LABORATORY

In 1974, Giorgini asked his colleague at Purdue, Wei-Chung Chen, to help develop Fortran code for Giorgini's mathematical model. In a report published by Purdue University entitled "Interfaces,"[8] Giorgini defined the innovative software, entitled Fields, as a "numerical visual laboratory." His choice of words here reflects his approach to the production of images by changing parameters of the program. These numerical parameters were not just variables of a mathematical equation; they were the ingredients to produce lines, points, and ellipses. In the document, Giorgini explains the relation between geometry, form, and experimentation: "Families of lines have a strong appeal to the imagination of anybody with [sic] inclination to geometrization. The gradual variation of curvature along each line from the other lines, constitute an infinite source of aesthetic possibilities for exploitation."[9]

Pieces made using Fields, are algorithmically produced from initial numerical values and plotted on paper at runtime. The *Interfaces* report (Figure 9) reveals in its sixty pages a complete description and source code of the software as well as Giorgini's artistic intentions for his computer art.

Moiré Patterns

CalComp could produce only lines, and Giorgini chose to fill in the shapes formed by the line intersections with checkerboard patterns. A talented painter with a steady hand, Giorgini filled in the small spaces between lines with the intent to create an optical experience for the viewer.[10] In "Interfaces," he explains his interest in the perceptual effects of his visual work: "When I first discovered this optical phenomenon, I tried to convince myself that it was just because my eyes were tired.

I showed the drawing to friends and visitors in order to check the accurateness of my observation."[11]

Giorgini described the resulting rippled designs as moiré patterns because they resulted from overlapping different patterns onto one another. He was strongly interested in the optical phenomena produced by intersecting lines and patterns in checkerboard patterns to enhance the moiré effect.[12] Black-and-white optic patterns became one of the most identifiable characteristics of Giorgini's visual art.

The moiré effect consists of a perceptual visual vibration caused by overlapping two or more patterns. This visual effect is oftentimes associated with the images perceived during psychedelic experiences. Gerald Oster, one of the most notable scientists who has investigated moiré patterns, examined this very phenomenon and explained the recurrence of visual vibration and geometric patterns during these psychedelic experiences. Oster conducted an experiment in which patients were exposed to repetitive groups of lines and concentric figures while on mescaline and LSD. The participants described that their experience of the moiré effect was heightened and that they perceived stronger visual vibrations. However, Oster rejected this association after discovering that these vibrations were actually due to involuntary eyeball movements.[13] The research concluded that moiré hallucinations were not exclusive to psychedelics. According to Oster, the same effect also could be achieved even by closing the eyes: "It is well known that in a restful mood prior to sleep and when the eyes are closed, visions of geometric patterns are seen. Children seem to 'see' them clearly. The literature on these 'visions' (phosphenes, as they are called) is quite extensive."[14]

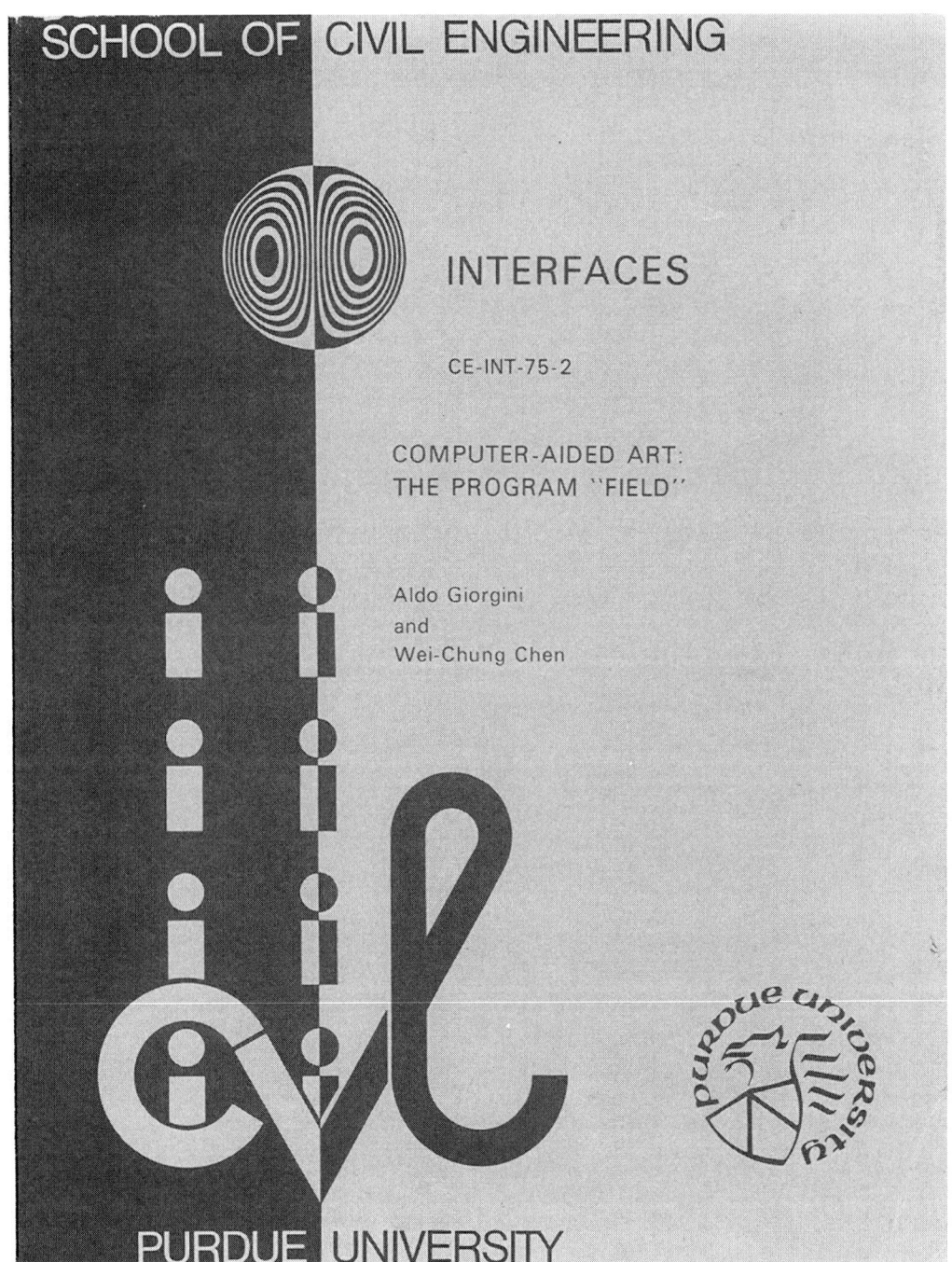

Figure 9. Cover design from the *Interfaces* report, 1975.

In a recent interview, curator Kit Basquin, an associate for administration at the Metropolitan Museum of Art in New York, described Giorgini's art: "It looked psychedelic. . . . Because if you don't know too much of electronic art, that's the only thing you can think of."[15]

Basquin formerly ran the Washington Gallery in the small town of Frankfort, Indiana. Giorgini supported Basquin's gallery program and visited gallery openings with his family. In 1973, Basquin provided Giorgini with his first venue to exhibit his computer art at the Washington Gallery. While Basquin was not particularly interested in curating computer art, she thought that Giorgini's "use of technology was original" and that his images were "very interesting, pleasant, and attractive." She also thought that he had a special control of algorithmic shape.[16] At this exhibition, Giorgini unveiled the results of his first studio experimentations using computers and other media. His first images were painted with India inks and markers.

In 1974, Aldo participated in another exhibit of computer art, which displayed his first experiments in addition to a new set of images created with Fields. The show was held at the Krannert Gallery at Purdue University.[17]

Giorgini first visualized his images conceptually and then modeled them with algorithms. He explained that, "In my particular case, when I am operating in the computer mode, I tend to fully prefabricate the images mentally and then to render them by computer."[18] His first designs, such as *Cybernethism, Arthropodics,* and *I Ain't a Spiral* were created in this way, each as a separate computer program. In contrast, *Negative Reflection* (Figure 10), *Turbulent Communications,* and *Claustrophobia* (Figure 11) used one single program—Fields. After experimenting with several codes, Giorgini found some constants, and he decided to write software that would allow him to compose images using vector primitives. The Fields software used prefabricated functions for points, ellipses, and rectangles. Figure 12 shows the geometrical design foundations of his piece *Claustrophobia.*

Visualizing the Z Dimension: A Mathematical Model

Giorgini's background in civil engineering and physics allowed him to use equipotential lines to produce contour lines. Some of the parameters of Fields are formulated in topographic terms. A piece produced by Fields can be described as a map view of mountains and valleys. A topographical representation in these two dimensions suggests a third dimension through the use of successive contour lines, which wrap around the different heights. Figure 13 shows a simplified circle-to-square transition.

Fields simulated physical terrains by producing a gradation of lines between surfaces of differing depth. The surfaces in Fields were named "boundaries," and they could be defined as points, ellipses, or circles. The program would create a field simulation that produced a series of contours around the "tallest" boundary toward the "lowest." The value of the depth at the boundaries was either *0* or *1*, and this was reflected in a variable named Z. The contour lines were produced as a transition from these two values. In the words of Giorgini, "the end product of the 'Operations performed on the elementary potential surfaces will closely resemble the geometrical representation of a physical field.'"[19]

The result was an image that represented the top view of simulated fields. The composition was defined by sets of points in Cartesian coordinates to produce geometric shapes. These shapes were considered to be at Z = 1 and would gradually transition to the boundary at Z = 0, producing the effect of the rippled contours. In Fields, the boundary at Z = 0 was typically a square that defined the aspect and border of the piece.

Print Portfolio

The "Interfaces" report served as an opportunity for Giorgini to create his first art portfolio. At his estate, approximately ten thousand letter-sized prints with the Fields images surfaced. Giorgini created the print portfolio by photographing cutouts of his work against a black background. The high-contrast images were taken to a printer and reproduced in a

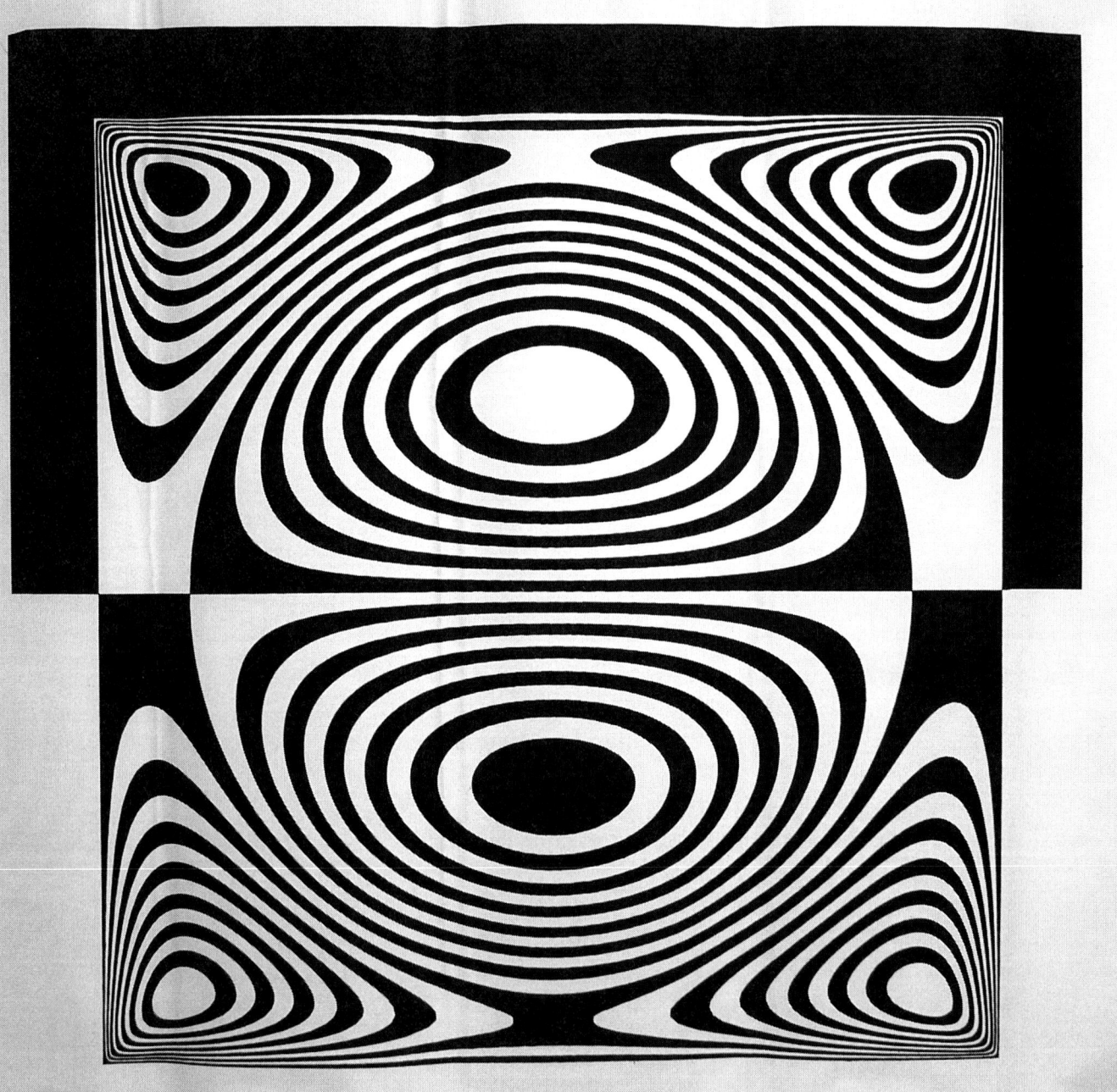

Figure 10. *Negative Reflection,* 1974. Screen print on linen, 40 x 40 in.

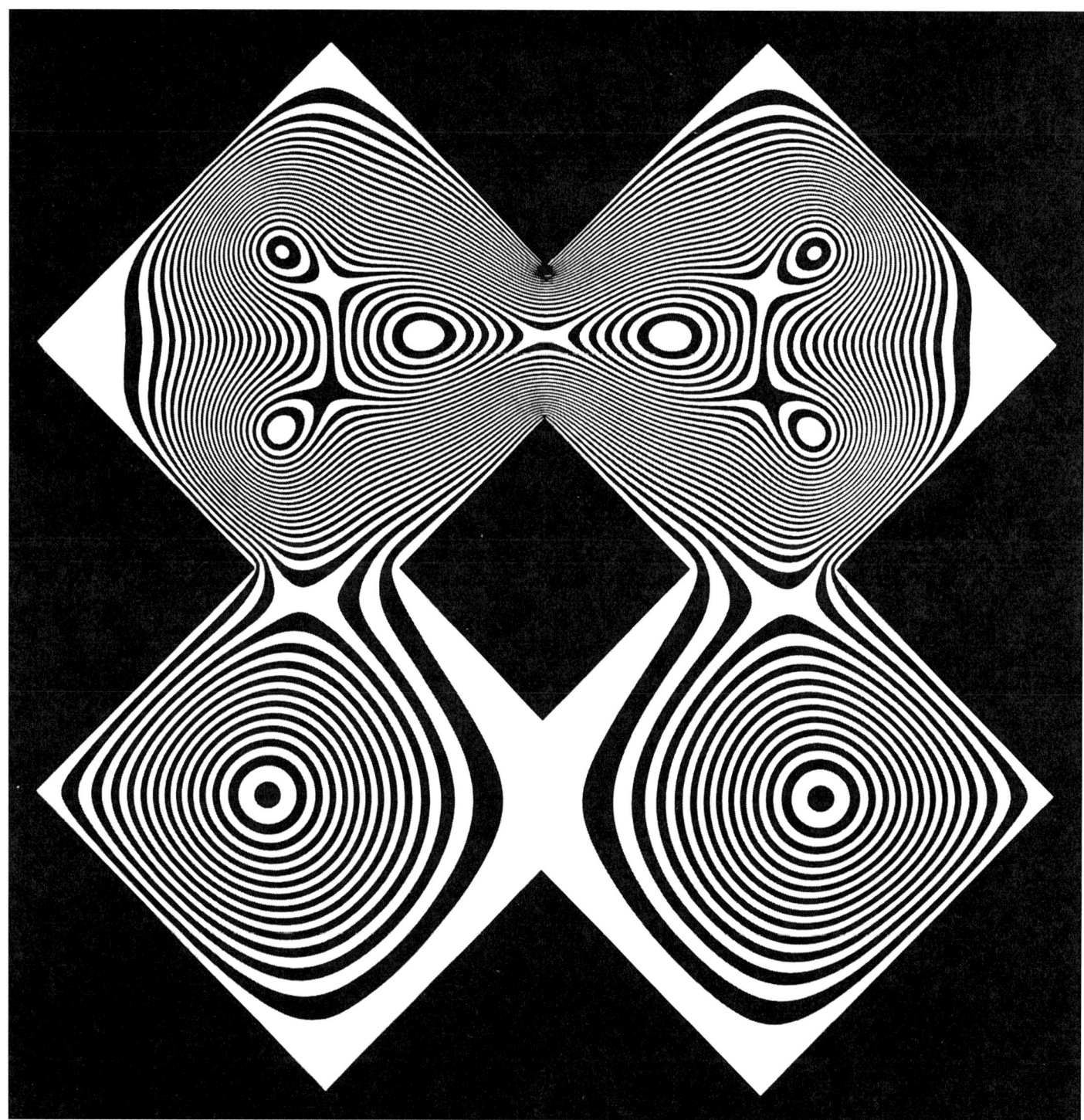

Figure 11. *Claustrophobia,*
1975. Offset print,
8 ½ x 11 in.

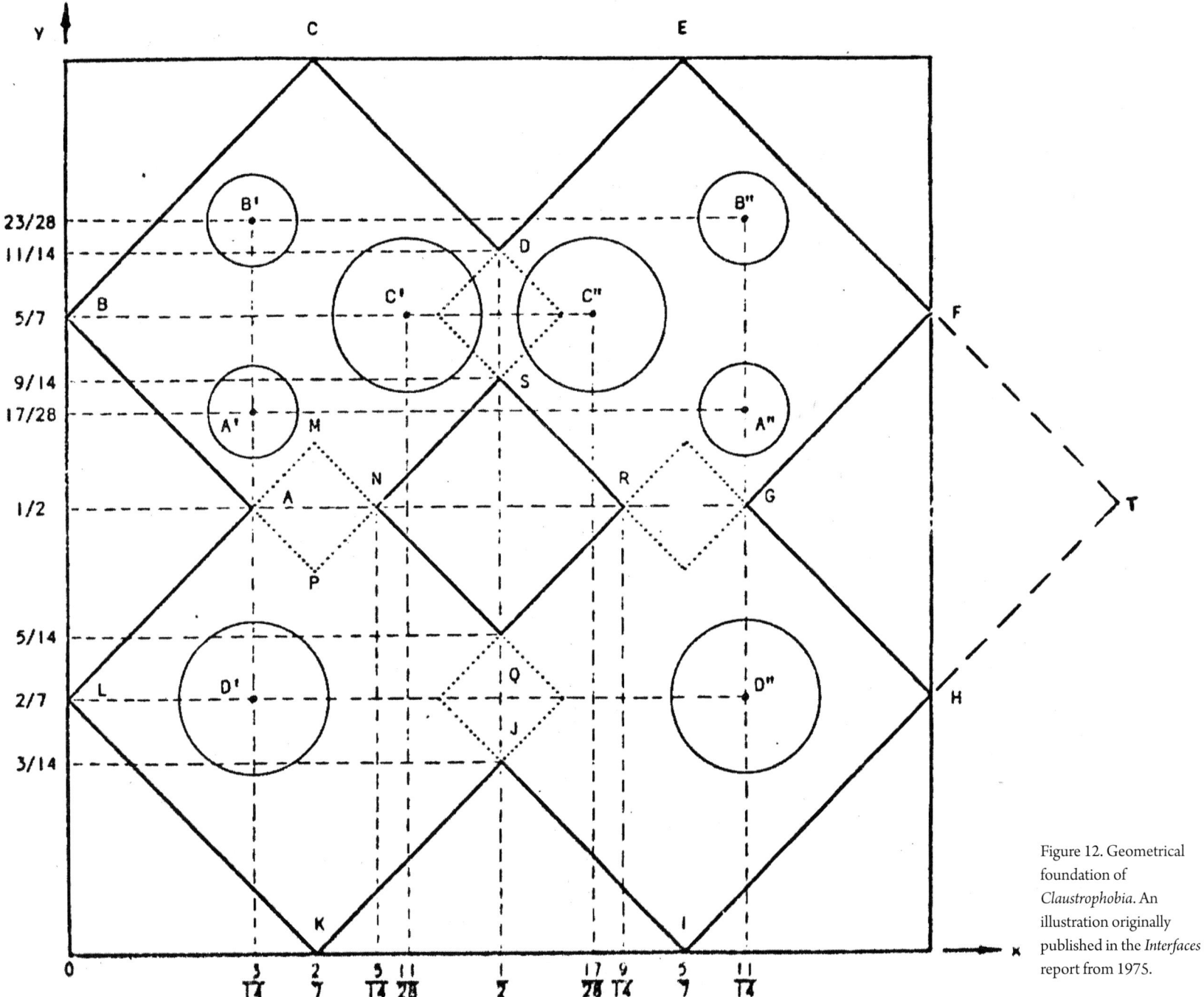

Figure 12. Geometrical foundation of *Claustrophobia*. An illustration originally published in the *Interfaces* report from 1975.

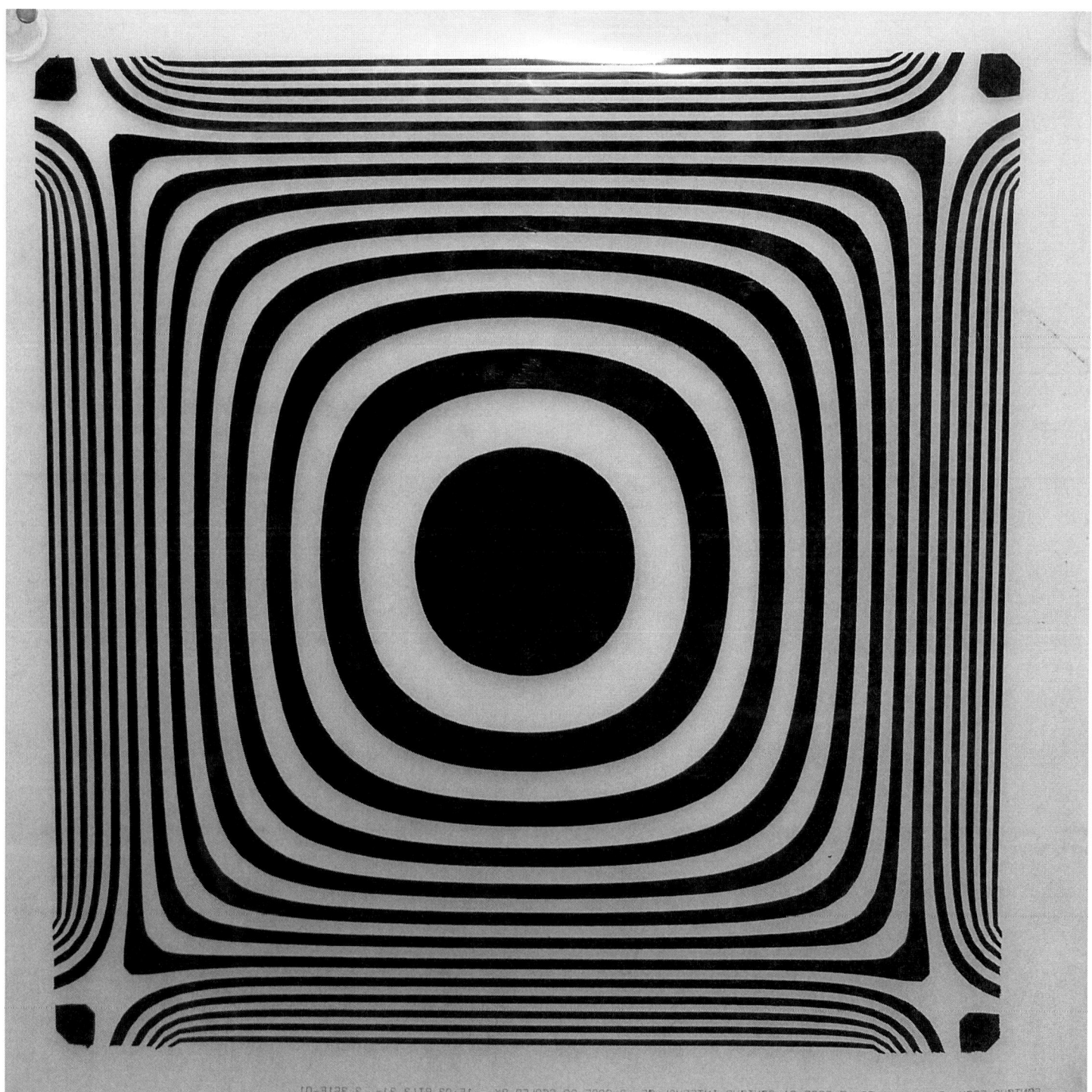

Figure 13. *Circle in Square,* 1974. Electrostatic print on Mylar, 36 x 36 in.

mechanic press. "Interfaces" included pages with the artwork as if it was an exhibition catalog. "Interfaces" and Fields were Giorgini's passport to fame in the world of computer art.

The images created using the software Fields continued to be exhibited throughout the 1970s and 1980s. His piece *Negative Reflection*, for example, was reprinted at a larger scale for the 1980 exhibit *Art In/Art Out* at the Ukrainian Institute of Modern Art in Chicago. Other Fields pieces, such as *The Kiss of Europa, Claustrophobia,* and *X*, also became representative of Giorgini's work, as they were published in a seminal book for computer art in 1976 entitled *Artist and Computer* by Ruth Leavitt. The images were reproduced from Giorgini's photographs of the paintings. He often used photography as means to reproduce or enlarge his work.

With this new body of work, Giorgini's "double career" as an artist and scientist became more apparent. After publishing the "Interfaces" report, Giorgini was established in the art world within an exclusive circle of artists creating art with computers. His devotion to computer art continued to grow over the years. His innovative 1974 solo exhibition at the Krannert Gallery raised the attention of the local press and placed Giorgini in the public sphere. The following chapters will describe Giorgini's transition from a professor conducting experiments with the computer to a renowned computer artist, and will discuss the distinctive work and processes that Giorgini used between 1975 and 1981. During that period he also created new software art frameworks such as *Surfaces, Light,* and *Stretch*. This was Giorgini's most prolific time, resulting in an extensive body of about one thousand large-scale artworks.

AESTHETICS IN TECHNOLOGY

Aldo Giorgini was interested in art not only as an artist, but also as an advocate. It was not unusual for him to be an active participant in a local art scene while simultaneously conducting scientific research. When he attended Colorado State as a postdoctoral fellow at the National Center for Atmospheric Research at Boulder, he also submitted gallery and film reviews to the local papers. Upon Giorgini's arrival at Purdue University in 1967, he connected with other artists and art enthusiasts across campus.

Giorgini's collaboration with the Purdue faculty included the Aesthetics in Technology Committee, comprised of professors from diverse engineering disciplines who wanted to bridge the gap between art and technology. The group had a special interest in bringing art to the A. A. Potter Engineering Center on campus. Among the works acquired by the committee were prints by Yves Tinguely and Frank Stella, as described in a faculty memorandum from May 1975.[20]

A facsimile found at Giorgini's estate documents the activities of this committee during 1974 and 1975. This sixty-page booklet, entitled *Aesthetics in Technology,* written by Giorgini, details a program by the same name. The document compiles transaction receipts, research reports, newsletters, and press clippings, and it reveals numerous activities that this committee performed. With the exception of one research project and a few interoffice memoranda, most of the publication is comprised of projects of Giorgini's direct involvement. Some of these projects included an artist-in-residence program, a research report on computational art titled "Surfaces," a symposium named "Computer Art Day," and a show titled *CE-X-hibit.*

Artist-in-Residence

Giorgini used the Aesthetics in Technology program as a catalyst for his own interests in furthering computer art. The activities allowed him to connect with an even larger computer art scene, this time beyond Indiana. A case in point was the artist-in-residence program, which brought to campus a diverse group of professional artists. The purpose of the program was described in the project's report from 1975: "To invite a nationally recognized U.S. artist to spend a 30 day period on the Purdue West Lafayette campus for the purpose of constructing a work of art and to interact with students and faculty in the schools of Engineering and in Creative Arts."[21]

The committee brought significant artists such as John David Mooney, who created a permanent installation for the Potter Center consisting of glass shapes that acted as cathode ray tubes. The work was on display at the Potter Center for thirty-seven years and is currently installed at the Electrical Engineering Building. Giorgini was the technical assistant for the visiting sculptors chosen by the committee; he gave them advice on Purdue University resources and materials that they could use to create their works.

Robert Mallary, who was formerly known as sculptor from the "neo-Dada" or "junk art" movement of the early 1960s,[22] began to create computer sculptures in 1968. Mallary was one of the first artists to use three-dimensional computing techniques to produce real objects. His approach was very similar to today's 3-D printers, in which an object is built by stacking layers of two-dimensional cut shapes. The gradual transition from shape to shape, stacking thin slices of plywood, "sculpted" the three-dimensional contours of the object. Mallary's TRAN2 computer graphics program allowed him to visualize and print each one of the slices. The designs were traced and cut in plywood, then stacked vertically.

During Mallary's residency at Purdue in 1974, he and Giorgini established a long-lasting friendship. Their affinity for the use of computers to make art led to a relationship beyond Purdue that introduced Giorgini to a new computer art community. Following Mallary's visit, he invited Giorgini to the University of Kansas in Lawrence to meet with Jeff and Colette Bangert.[23] Jeff worked at the University of Kansas Computer Center from 1965 to 2000. He is a mathematician who in 1959 married Colette, a lifelong visual artist. Together they dialogued art and science leanings through their computer art collaboration.

In 1974, Colette led a panel on computer art at the Mid-America College of Art Association Conference (MACAA) in DeKalb, Illinois, at Northeastern Illinois University. She invited Giorgini and the renowned artist and physicist Kenneth Knowlton to participate. Giorgini presented his work made with the Fields software in a presentation called "Un-Canned Computer Art Program."

"Computer Art Day"

The MACAA experience inspired Aldo to create a similar forum for computer art, using the resources that he had available through the Aesthetics in Technology program. In a recent interview, Bangert recalled Giorgini's motivation to organize a computer art symposium that gathered artists from around the United States: "Aldo got the idea and talked with people at Purdue to organize a symposium that was focused in computers and art. Aldo got his university to sponsor this and asked me to help him. He and I worked on who to invite and how to plan the event. So we all went from all over the country."[24]

The symposium was entitled "Computer Art Day" and took place in March 1975. This event brought to the Purdue campus some of the most relevant computer artists of that time, such as Charles Csuri, Kurt Lauckner, Jeff and Colette Bangert, Robert Mallary, Richard Helmick, Lillian Schwartz, and Harold Cohen. A clipping from the local Lafayette newspaper (Figure 14) published during the event stated, "Artists and scientists from throughout the nation will be represented at the full day symposium and nine artists will discuss aspects of the computer's role in the visual arts and display drawings, paintings and sculpture at the session."[25] Another newspaper quoting Giorgini explained the focus of the symposium: "The computer's role in the visual arts is that of a powerful, but complex medium of artistic expression. The complexity of the tool and the facility of its graphical outputs have led to either innocent or intentional missuses."[26] In a taped recording from the symposium, Mallary explained

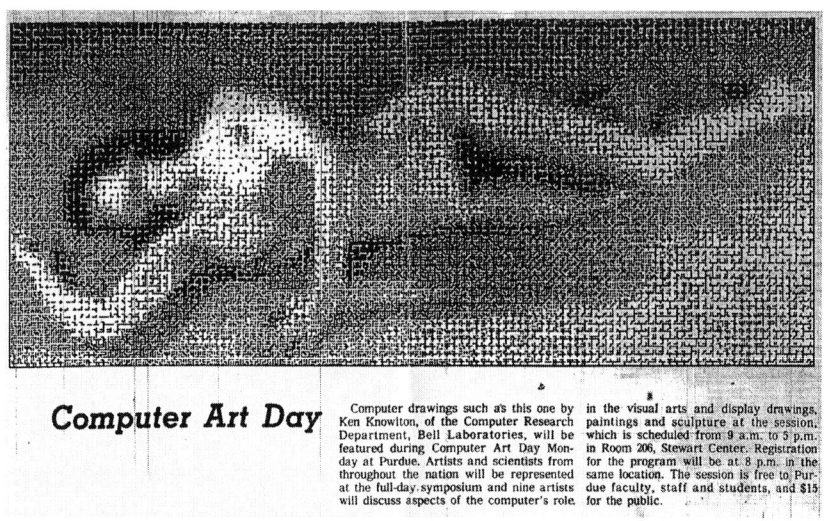

Computer Art Day Computer drawings such as this one by Ken Knowlton, of the Computer Research Department, Bell Laboratories, will be featured during Computer Art Day Monday at Purdue. Artists and scientists from throughout the nation will be represented at the full-day symposium and nine artists will discuss aspects of the computer's role. in the visual arts and display drawings, paintings and sculpture at the session, which is scheduled from 9 a.m. to 5 p.m. in Room 206, Stewart Center. Registration for the program will be at 8 p.m. in the same location. The session is free to Purdue faculty, staff and students, and $15 for the public.

Figure 14. Local news clipping displaying the work of Ken Knowlton and Leon Harmon, "Computer Art Day," *Journal and Courier* (Lafayette, IN), March 22, 1975, courtesy of Tippecanoe County Library Archives.

the importance of academic settings in the development of the new discipline of computer art. He described "the university as an environment, a resource, and a system for the support of computer art," speaking from his personal experience at the University of Massachusetts Amherst.[27]

Giorgini's friendship with Mallary and the Bangerts continued through a series of exhibitions across the United States between 1974 and 1986. Several letters describe either Mallary's or the Bangerts' recommendation of Giorgini for new computer art venues. This was the case with several exhibits, such as the *Computer Art Exhibit* at University of Iowa in 1984, curated by Jackie Lipsky.[28]

After the symposium at Purdue, Giorgini became recognized among colleagues who were practitioners of computer art in the United States. It is not an accident that his work was included in a seminal book of computer art, *Artist and Computer*.[29] The book had the important task of documenting many of the computer artists who were active at that time. *Artist and Computer* collected essays by artists from around the world who used the computer as an art tool. Ruth Leavitt submitted a letter with ten questions to a pool of artists, asking them about their computer art practice. Her book gathered thirty-five responses from significant international computer artists such as Manuel Barbadillo, a Spanish art professor whose work resembles Giorgini's visual style. The artists featured in this publication were pioneers in making art with computers long before the personal computer era. Giorgini's four-page essay is complemented with some images produced using the Fields software. In addition to the Fields work, *Artist and Computer* shows a newer colorful design also created by Giorgini. The centerfold of the book reveals a stretched flag design. The stretching of two-dimensional surfaces through the use of algorithms became Giorgini's new pastime.

STRETCHED SURFACES

From 1975 to 1977, Giorgini's new artistic focus became stretching two-dimensional surfaces. In a report from his research, Giorgini explains his intent of manipulating surfaces using computer graphics techniques. His idea of "visual experiments on surfaces" [30] consisted of projecting two-dimensional images into three-dimensional planes. At first, he created the surface as a mathematical formula:

$$Surface\ z = xy(1\text{-}x)(1\text{-}y)$$

In computer graphics, an image can be defined as a two-dimensional function of width and height. Giorgini mapped a two-dimensional function expressed in $xy(1\text{-}x)(1\text{-}y)$ to a three-dimensional function by adding the parameter z. By doing this, he developed an algorithm to visualize two-dimensional images in three dimensions, as if the plane was a blanket waving in space. Giorgini called this surface equation Ravioli, revealing his playful attitude toward his artistic experiments.

It was common for Giorgini to add a third dimension to his mathematical models to distort images by either stretching them or contracting them. Ravioli, for example, is the foundation of a series of twenty-seven different artworks, including *Stripes*, *Checkerboard* (Figure 15), *Swiss Cheese* (Figure 16), and *Polka Dots*. These works were installed at Purdue's civil engineering building at the end of the 1975 spring semester, only a few weeks after the "Computer Art Day" symposium. *CE-X-hibit* featured Giorgini's work and his students' projects from his course entitled "Aesthetics in Civil Engineering Design." As seen in Figure 17, mural-like installations made with his prints decorated the hallways of the civil engineering building.

Giorgini brought his algorithmic compositions created at Purdue to his art studio, experimenting with ways of creating large-scale multiple images. He used his own spacious basement to create huge paintings and prints. A table in the center of a room was used to meticulously fill in with paint the characteristic surfaces that resulted from overlapping computer plots with lines. About one thousand works produced during 1975 and 1981 that were found at Giorgini's home show his dedication to his studio practice. During this period, Giorgini explored three distinct methods of image production and reproduction: electrostatic print, screen print, and photomontage. Although they were different processes, all of them involved the initial step of painting black over computer-plotted images.

Electrostatic Print

Giorgini's work started with creating algorithmic lines on the computer. The resulting images were then plotted in a thirty-six-inch paper roll using a CalComp plotter. It is for this reason that the majority of Giorgini's work has this width as a consistent measure, even when he created larger pieces resulting from connecting several thirty-six-inch modules.

The computer plots with lines were taken to the Purdue Print Shop, a copy center located in Stewart Center. Large-format electrostatic printers introduced in the 1970s had only two options: printing on paper or Mylar. The device used a heated transfer of fine carbon particles into the media similarly to modern toner-based printers and copiers. [31] Giorgini used both media for different purposes. The photocopied CalComp plot in Mylar was painted onto its matte surface and black acrylic or India ink

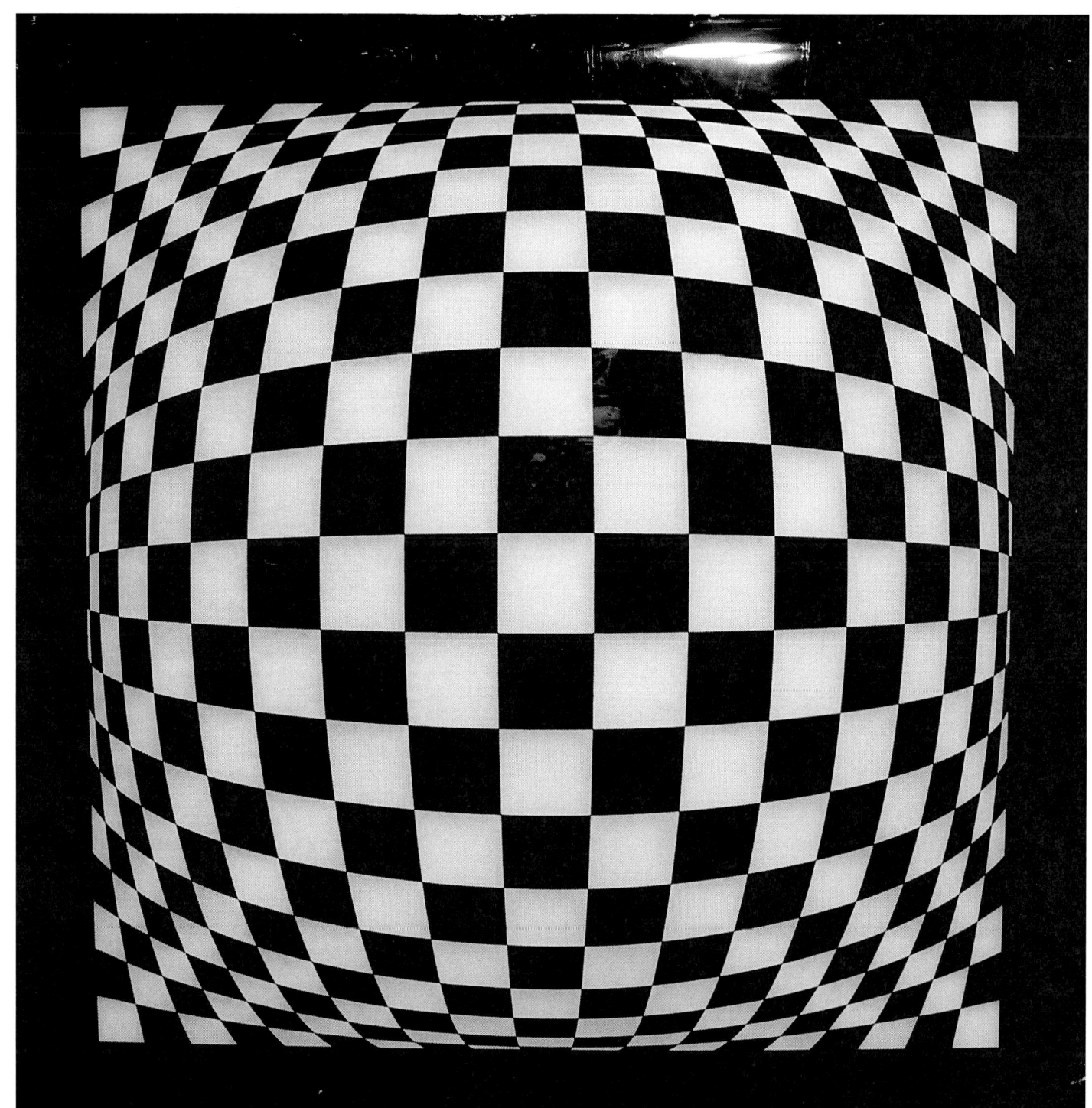

Figure 15. *Checkerboard*, 1975. Electrostatic print on Mylar, 36 x 36 in.

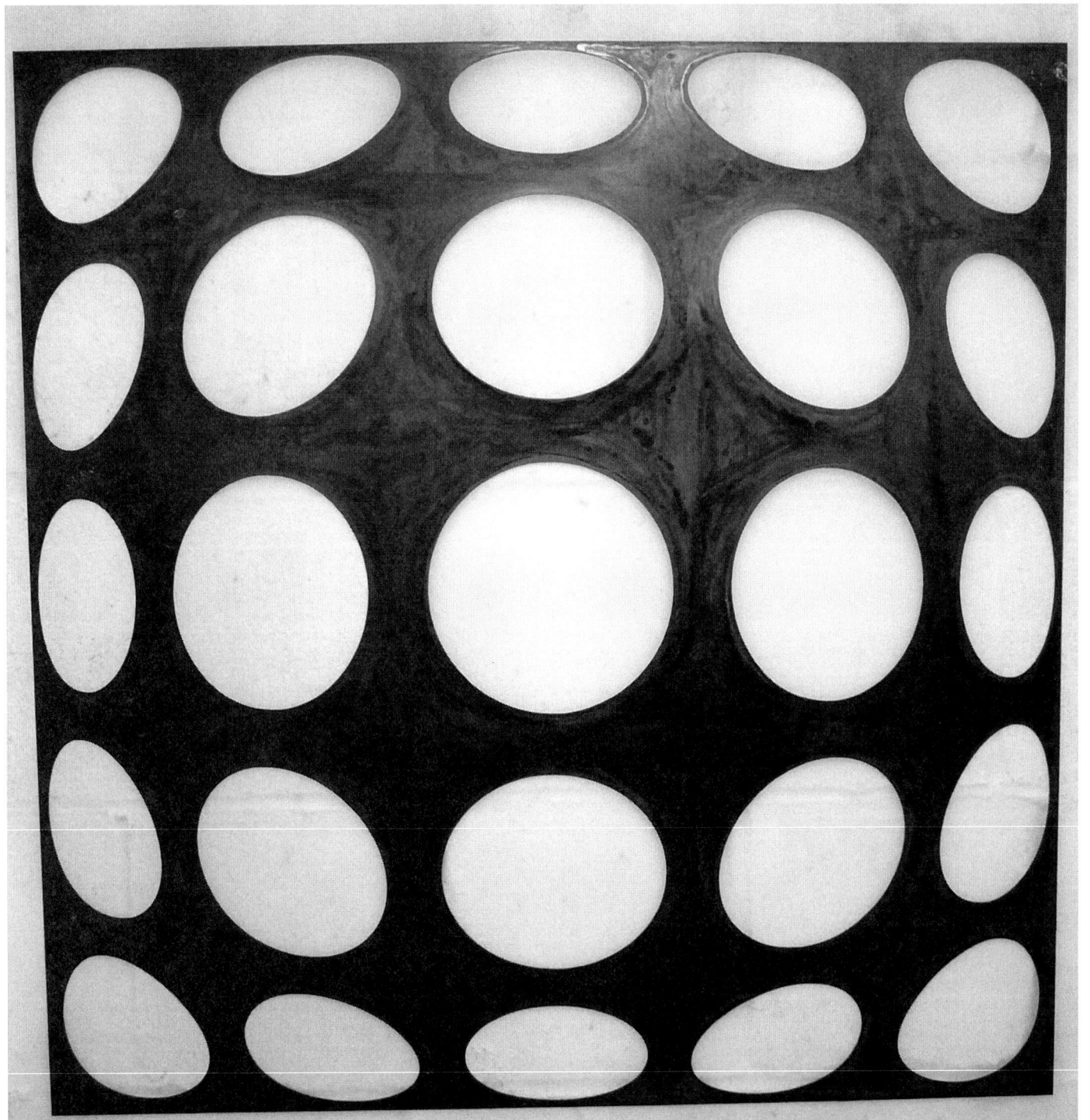

Figure 16 (left). *Swiss Cheese,* 1975. Acrylic paint on Mylar, 36 x 36 in.

Figure 17 (right). *Stripes* installed at CE-X-hibit in 1975. Photograph.

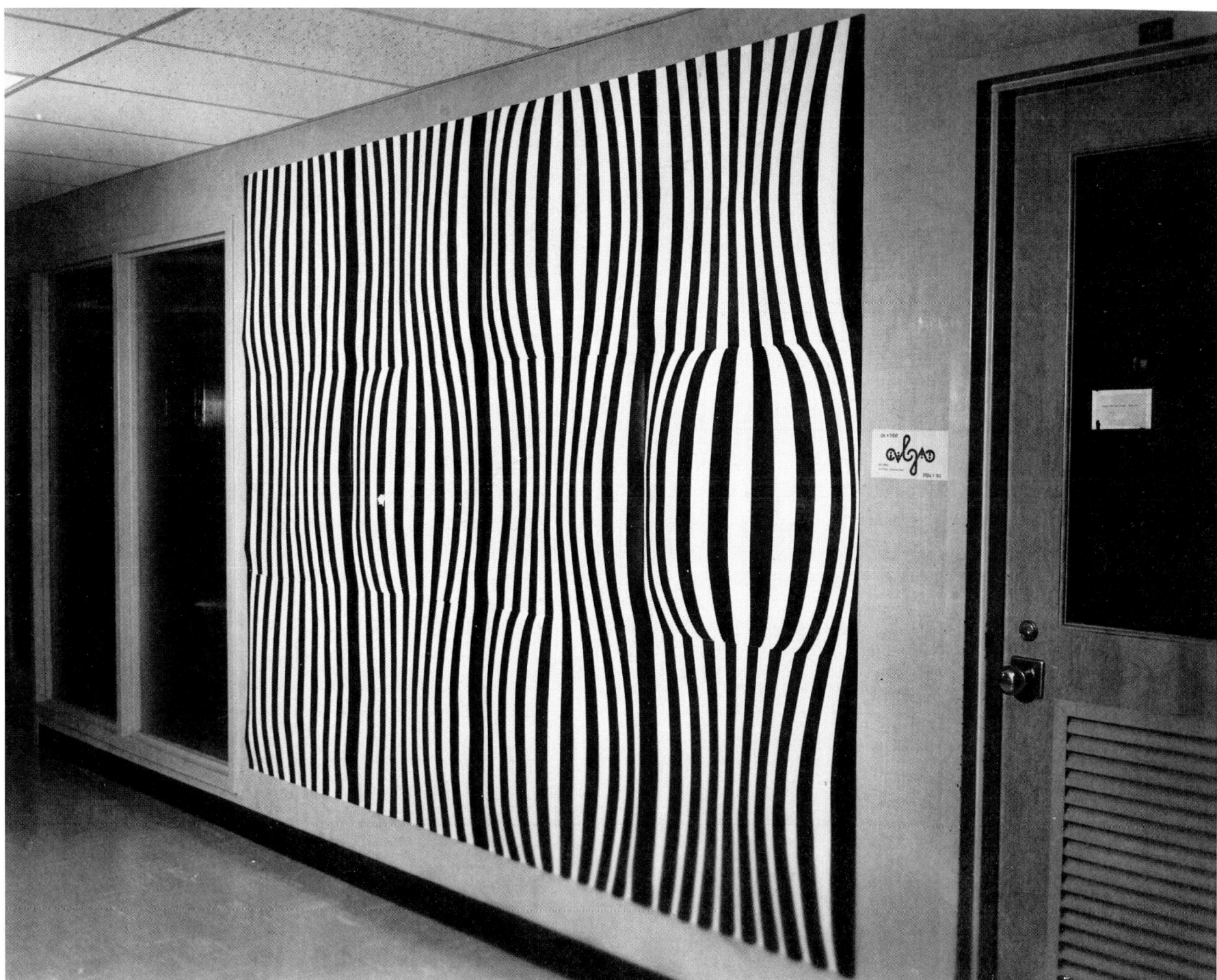

was used to fill in shapes. The thirty-six-inch-wide painted Mylar pieces ranged from thirty-six to one hundred inches long, a significant dimension for painting. Some of the Mylar prints were signed, numbered, and exhibited in other venues, but the majority of the 280 original paintings are practically unknown and remained at Giorgini's estate. Giorgini used the paper copies to make art installations like the ones in *CE-X-hibit*. A flood in the early 2000s damaged a large number of the electrostatic prints on paper, but the Mylar paintings and prints survived the humid conditions in which they were immersed for thirty years. It is fortunate that Giorgini used a polyethylene-based film as the support for his paintings.

A common element found in Giorgini's computer artworks from this period is the use of geometrically modeled cylinders interrupting fluid flow. An article in the *Indianapolis Star Magazine* from 1977 explains Giorgini's affinity for exploring fluid mechanics with an artistic intent: "Although its effect is obvious, no one knows exactly what happens when water (or any other liquid) starts moving. What and how forces are generated in a whirlpool or as flood waters swirl around cylindrical pilings and a host of other questions involving unseen forces in moving liquids are mysteries. So, Giorgini is applying engineering techniques with artistic principles to seek the answer."[32]

Examples of his experiments with cylinders include *Perturbation of a Connector Flow* (Figure 18), *Cylinder Ozeen* (Figure 19), *Streams and Whirls, Oozen Relative, Oozen Vorticity, Flow Around Two Cylinders, Ideal Flow* (Figure 20), *Sculptural Forms,* and *Fiat Lux*.[33] Giorgini was able to create multiple image sequences simulating different moments of the interrupted fluid flow. Each one of the aforementioned titles belong to series with different variations of the same work. For example, *Perturbation of a Connector Flow* consists of an image sequence of nine surfaces with uniform ripples that gradually become turbulent.

After copying the finished painting through the electrostatic process, Giorgini achieved prints that had solid black shapes, removing the traces of his handmade process.[34] The purpose of clearing away imperfections was to enhance the optical effects that his paintings produced in the viewer's mind. Giorgini states in the *Indianapolis Star Magazine* that "the hand can entirely butcher a design drawing if you are interested in very subtle patterns like moiré patterns."[35] The painting results were sometimes not satisfactory for Giorgini. He redid entire meticulous paintings because of a small ink smear or a mismatch in the alternating pattern.

Screen Print

By having perfectly uniform black shapes, Giorgini was also able to use his designs for screen printing. Giorgini used emulsion-based silkscreen frames coated and developed in a dark room of his studio since 1974. A screen print frame with the *Cybernethism* design is shown in Figure 21. A recent interview with Massimiliano provides an explanation for Giorgini's screen printing process. Massimiliano recalled his father printing the *Surfaces* portfolio in their home's driveway in Lafayette, using a squeegee and different two-color combinations.[36]

The serigraph portfolio was part of a limited edition of 135 works and featured the designs that were developed during his research for *Visual Experiments on Surfaces* (Figure 22). Giorgini started by using the Ravioli formula to create design variations within the same pattern. He chose to juxtapose two images from the *Stripes* series and used gray and black ink on paper to make *Folio 1* and *Folio 2*. A screen printed cardboard folio held the five 20-inch-by-26-inch prints with the title *Surfaces*. The overlapping patterns of different colors made the surfaces look as if they were three-dimensional ribbons that whirled and looped in the space. His decision to use two colors enhanced the effect of more depth; the addition of a secondary color represented the back of the same surfaces.

Giorgini used a rippled flag design to create the remaining images in the portfolio. The work *Flag* consists of seven vertical ribbons. He also filled in the backside of the three-dimensional ribbons and alternated the

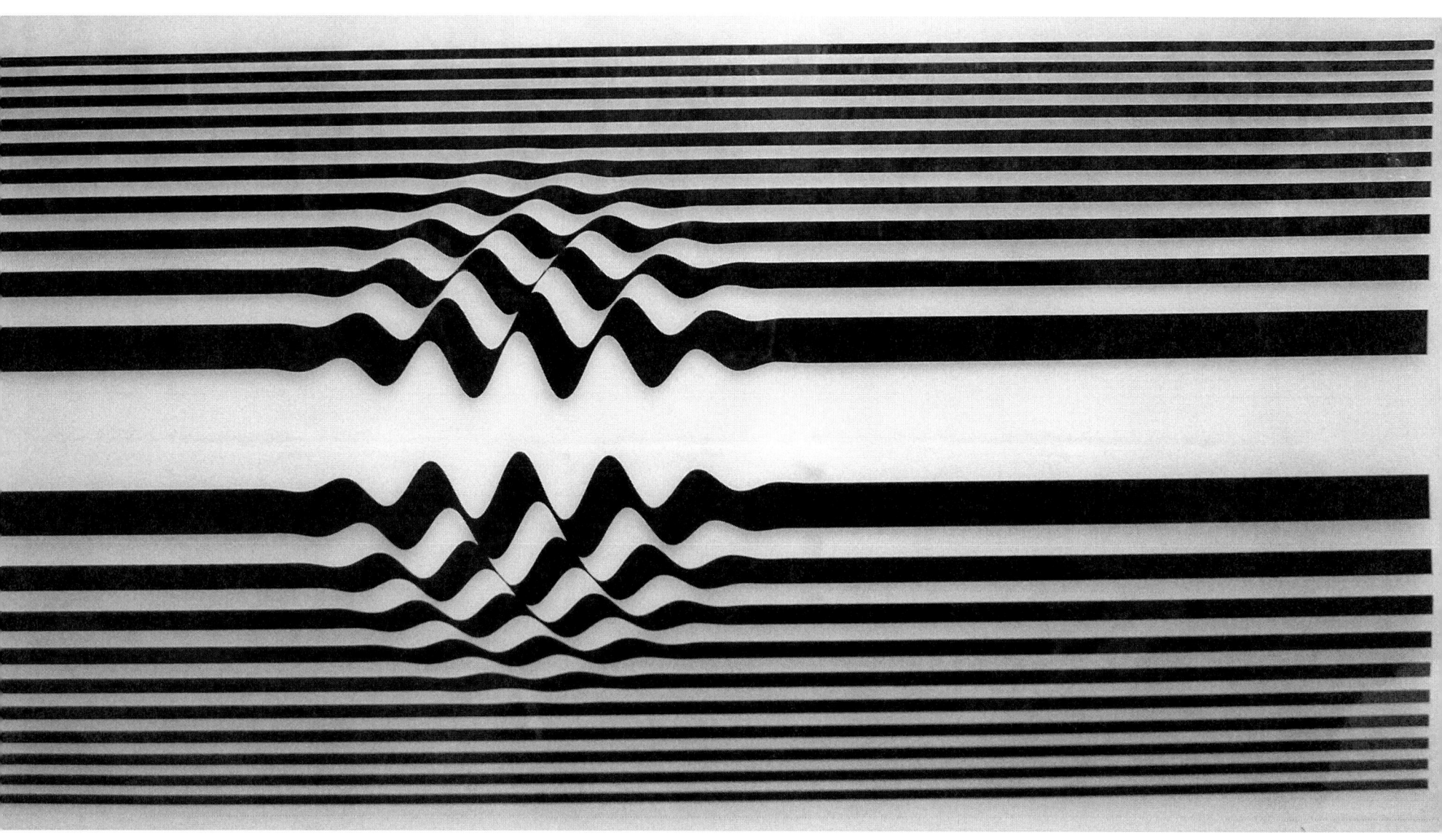

Figure 18. *Perturbation of a Connector Flow,* 1975. Electrostatic print on Mylar, 57 x 36 in.

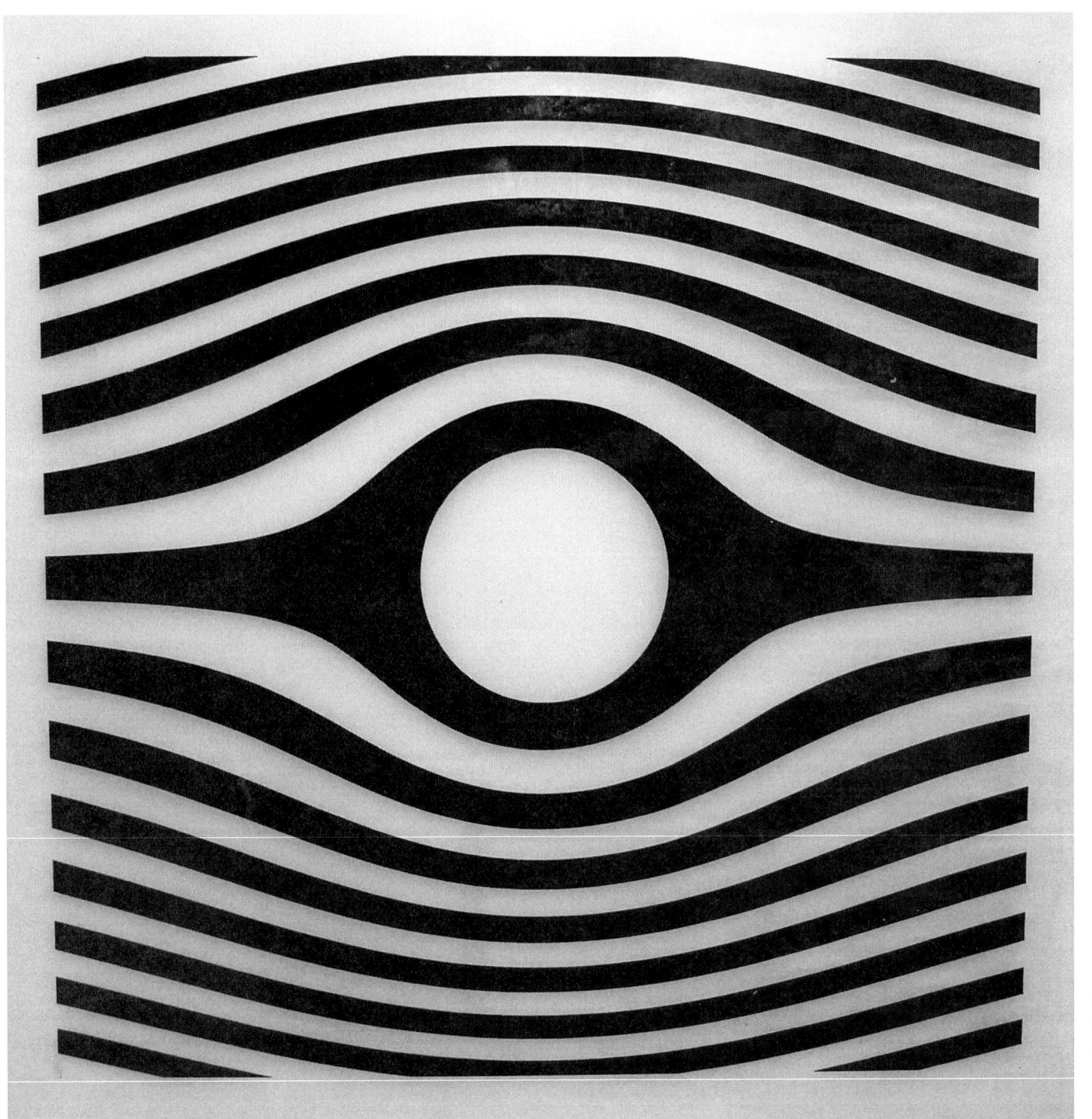

Figure 19. *Cylinder Ozeen*, 1976.
Electrostatic print on Mylar,
36 x 36 in.

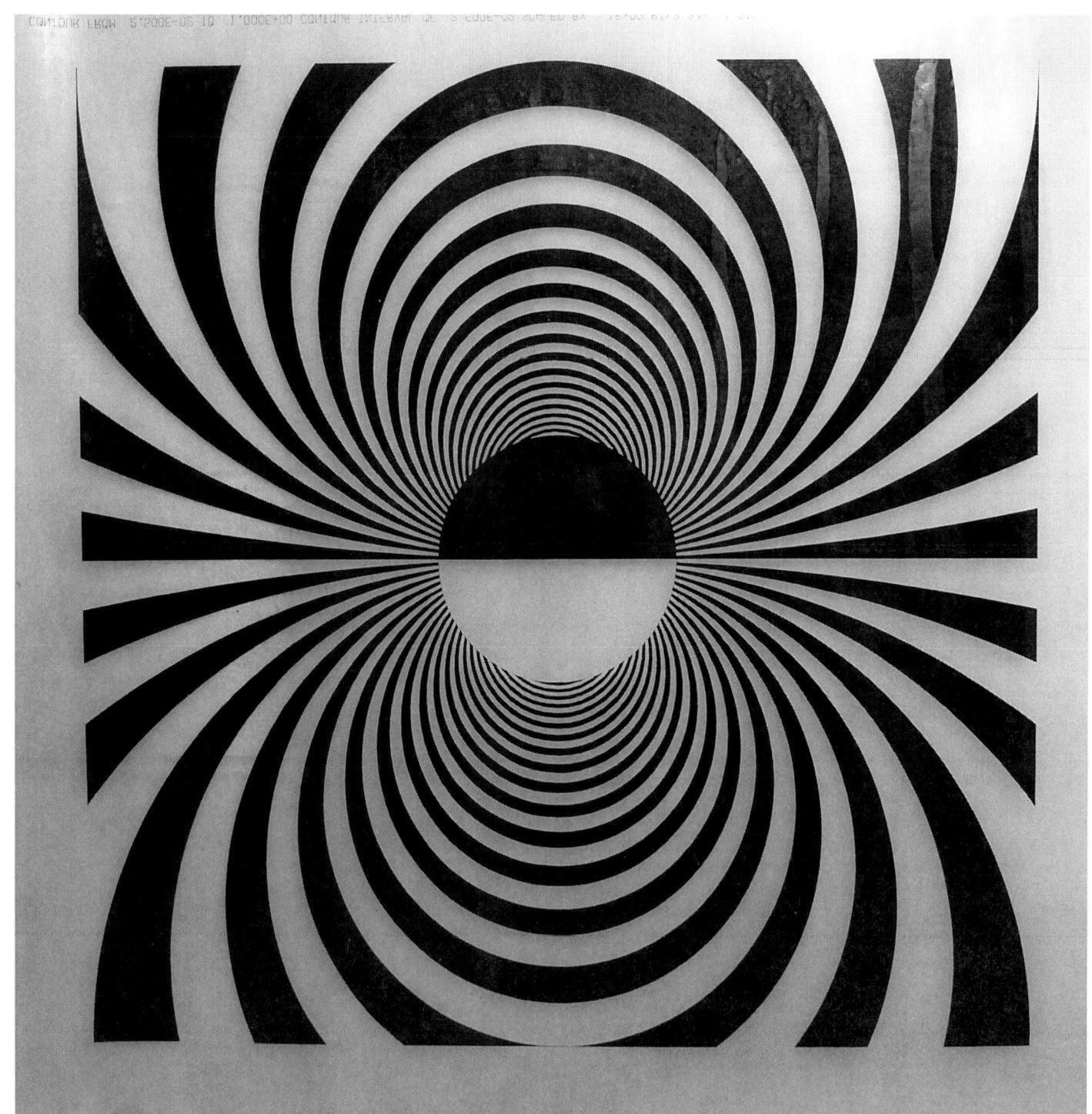

Figure 20. *Ideal Flow,* 1976.
Electrostatic print on Mylar,
36 x 36 in.

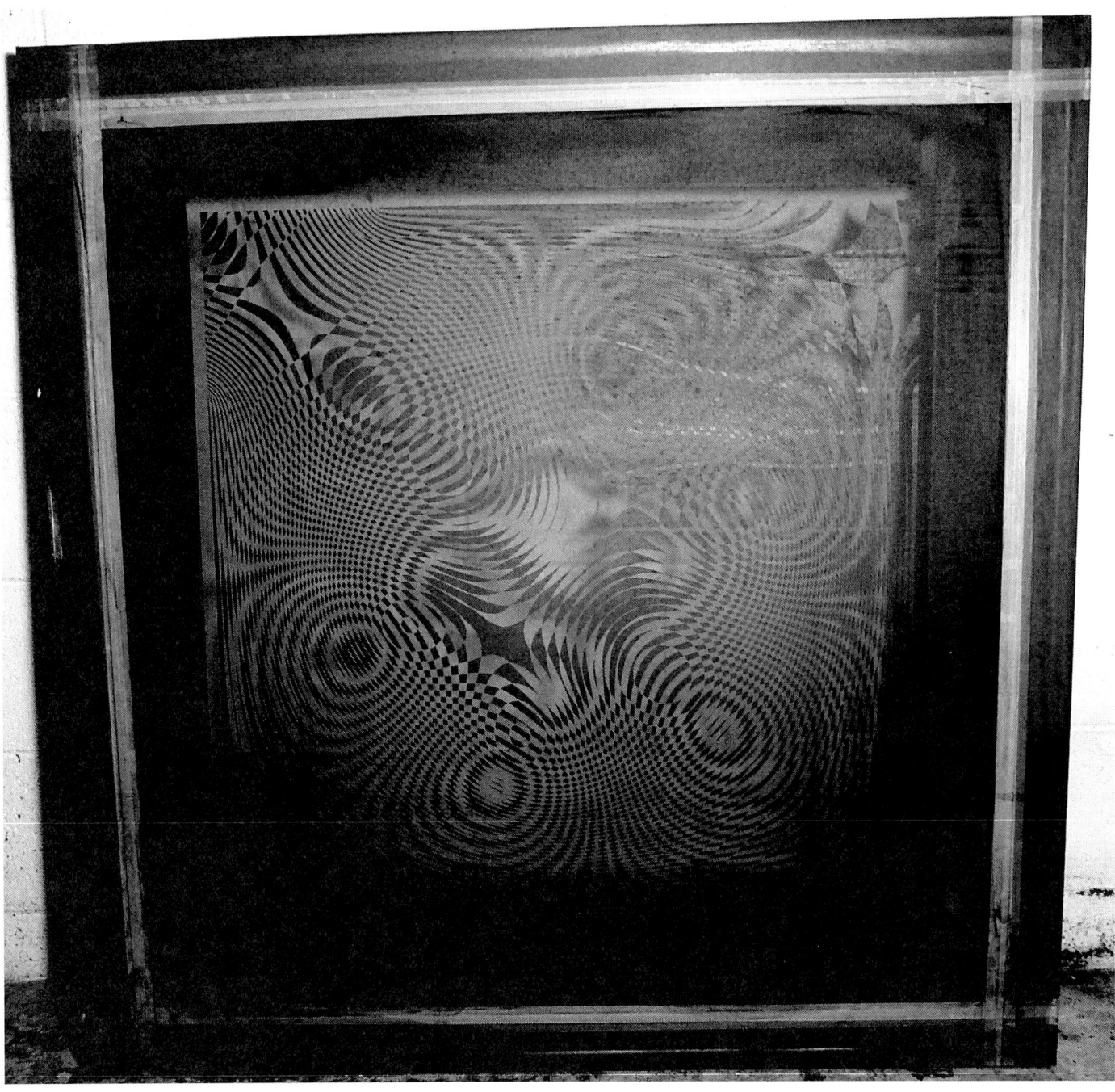

Figure 21. *Cybernethism* design on a 40 x 40 in. screenprint frame. Δ Courtesy of Aldo Giorgini's estate.

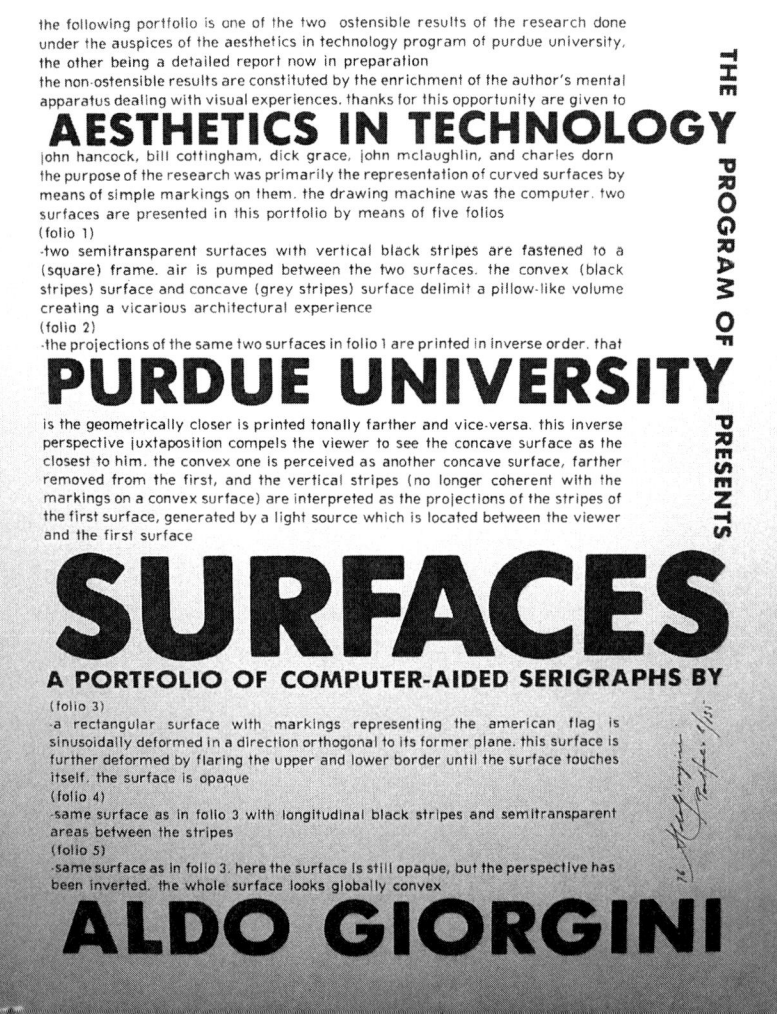

Figure 22. *Surfaces*: Signed portfolio cover with art statement. Screen-print on paper, 20 x 26 in.

colors and the order in which he screen printed. Giorgini was interested in how the surfaces were perceived differently by viewers: "This inverse perspective juxtaposition compels the viewer to see the concave surface as the closest to him. The convex one is perceived as another concave surface farther removed from the first."[37] *Folio 4* and *Folio 5* (Figures 23 and 24) show the mentioned visual effect of perceiving the same design differently by changing the colors of the shapes printed.

Folio 3 used the same foundation of the rippled flag, but as seen in Figure 25, Giorgini appropriated the United States flag in a pop art form. In *American Flag*, Giorgini applied his stretching techniques to the iconic flag and added a rectangular shape with algorithmically distorted stars in its upper-left corner. The work was printed using blue and red inks to resemble the original colors of the symbol. At Giorgini's estate, an unusual print with the same design surfaced, showing the flag printed on black paper with green and orange inks. Giorgini's intent was to create the "after-image" optical effect, in which a person can construct an image in his or her mind after looking at its negative colors. According to Massimiliano, his father did not like the visual results of the after-image flag,[38] so it was never distributed. The flag piece was intended to be a statement of gratitude from the Italian-born artist and scientist; after having spent his childhood as a World War II refugee in Eritrea, Giorgini was able to pursue his intellectual goals in the United States. Multiple copies of *American Flag* remain at Giorgini's estate, along with a 1990 limited edition of *American Flag* T-shirts and sweatshirts that Giorgini distributed among his friends, family, and colleagues.

The signed and numbered print portfolios contain what is probably Giorgini's most exhibited work. *Surfaces* was acquired by art institutions that added it to their permanent collections for preservation and public display. These institutions include Lehigh University, the Carnegie Museum of Art, the Art Museum of Greater Lafayette, University Galleries at the Ohio State University, Indianapolis Museum of Art, and the

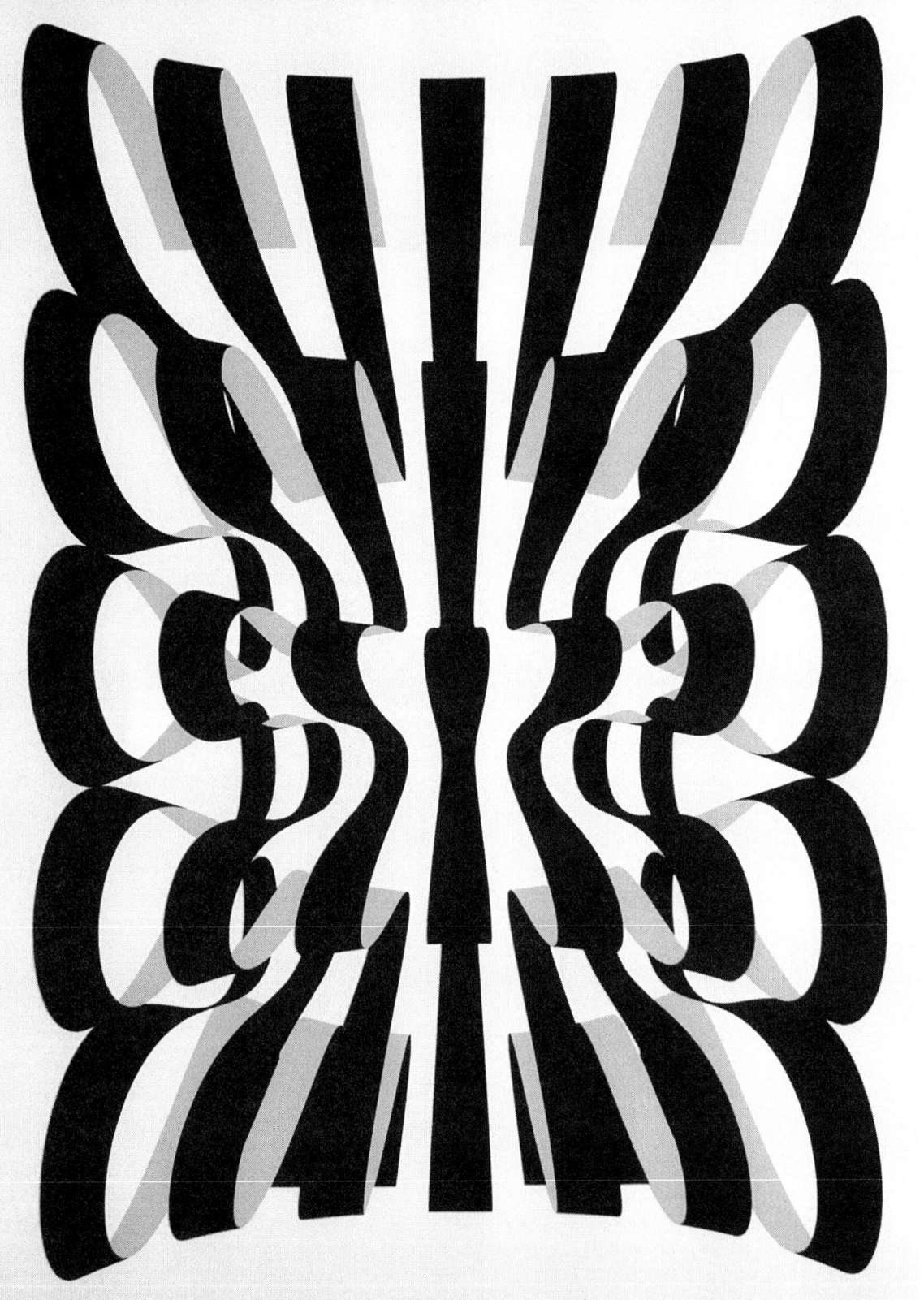

Figure 23. *Surfaces: Folio 4,*
1976. Screen-print on paper,
20 x 26 in.

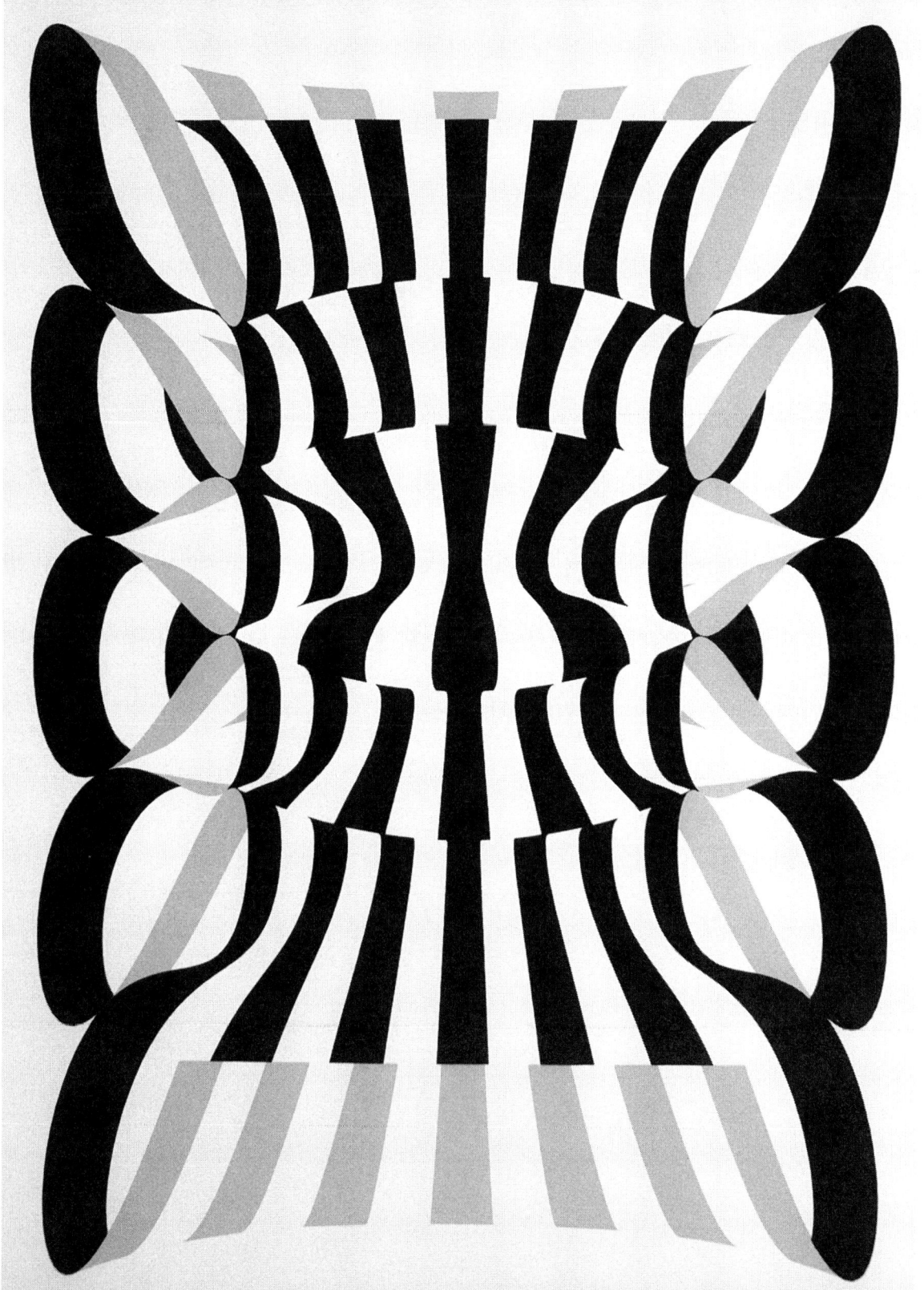

Figure 24. *Surfaces: Folio 5,*
1976. Screen-print on paper,
20 x 26 in.

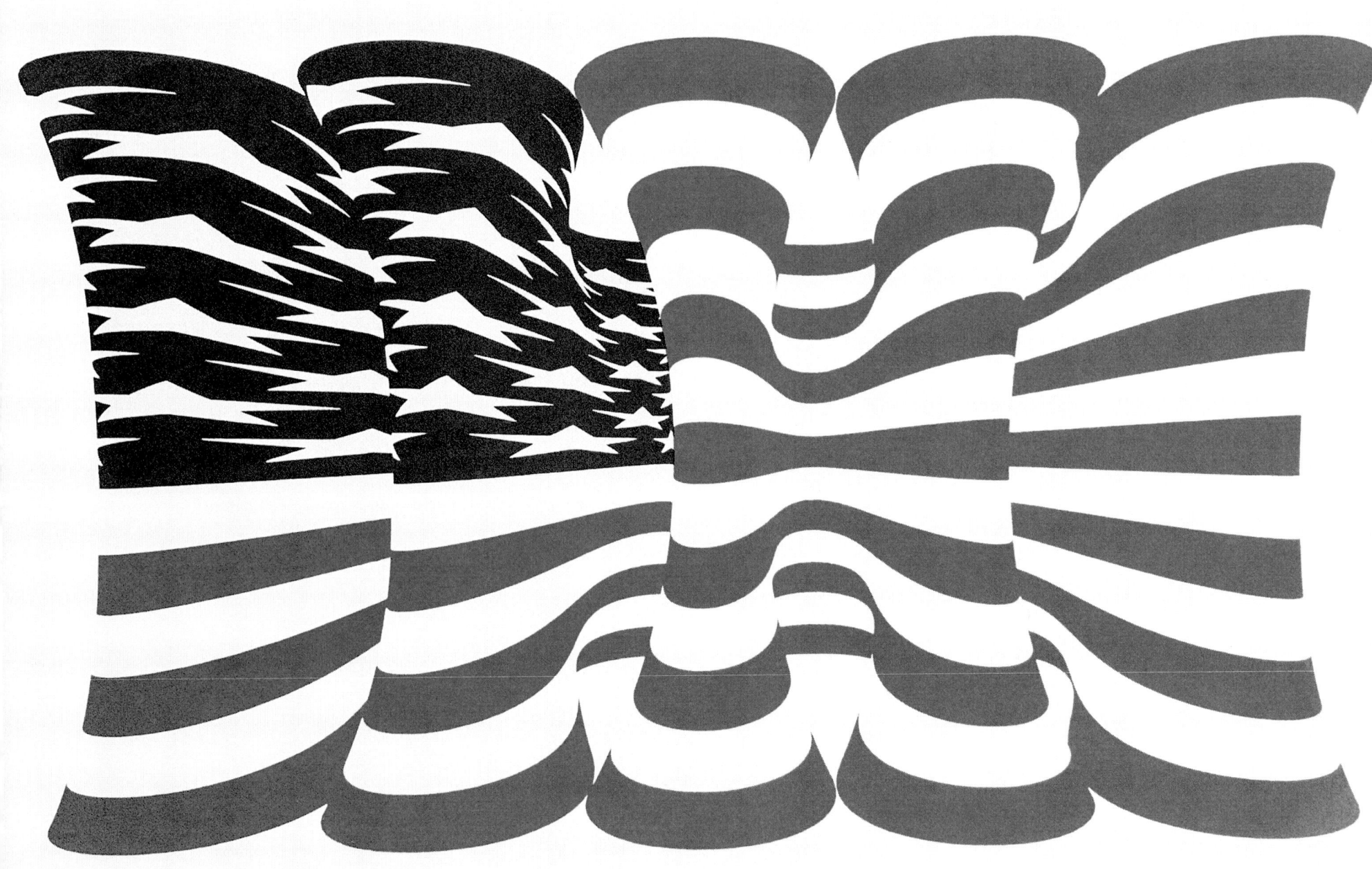

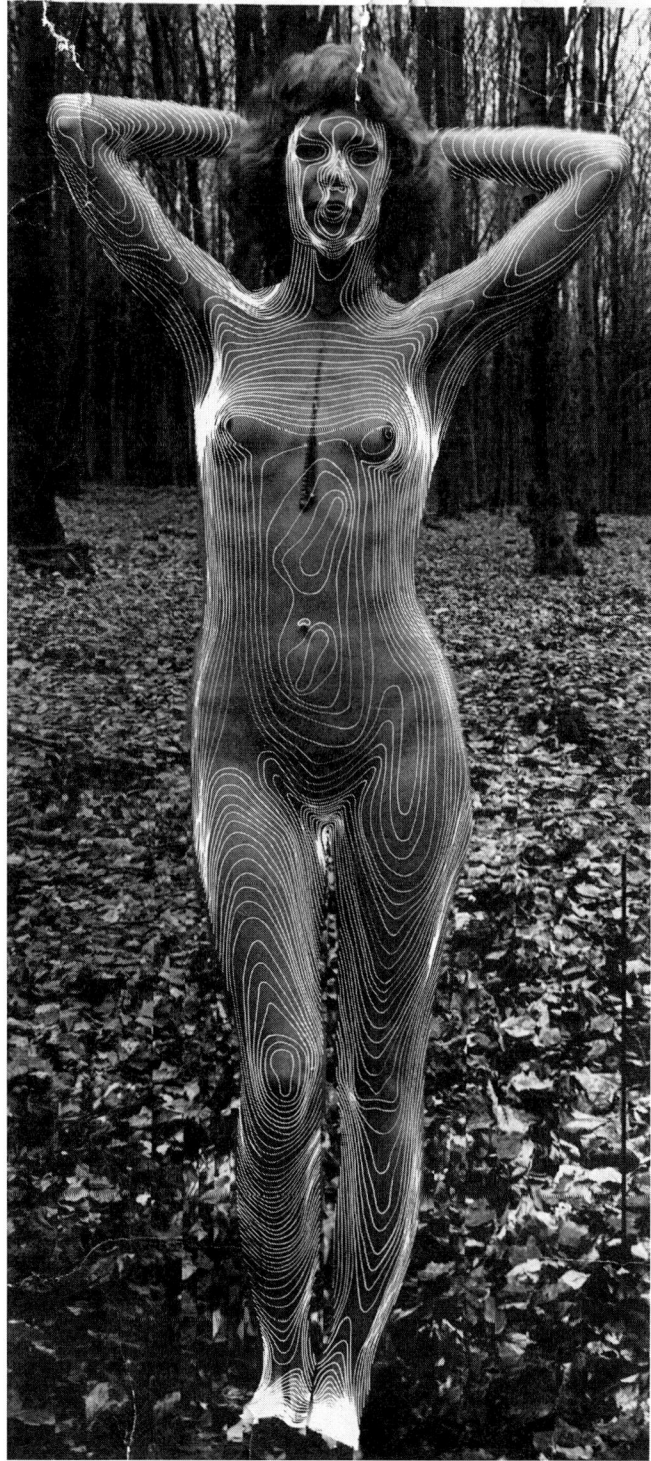

National Collection of Fine Arts from the Smithsonian Institution in Washington, DC, to name a few.

Photomontage

The Aesthetics in Technology committee commissioned Giorgini to create a permanent installation of his work at the Potter Center. So, in 1976, Giorgini started to work on an artistic software called Light. The new program was capable of simulating virtual lights in a geometric space. Groups of lines depict a zenithal view of light and dark surfaces. Giorgini was able to change the numerical intensity of his programmed, theoretical lights and make them interact in his program. Another new feature was that Light could create an image in separated modules. The once limiting width of thirty-six inches became just a fragment of a larger image. Using this method in conjunction with a photographic process, Giorgini produced the murals *Sculptural Forms* and *Fiat Lux*.

After *Surfaces*, Giorgini became more comfortable with the creation and manipulation of shapes through the use of algorithms. In contrast with his earlier work, Light enriched a visual vocabulary of surfaces that Giorgini could model at his will. His first experiments with photomontage are documented in a photograph layered with computer-aided shapes. The work depicts a nude woman decorated with computer-plotted lines that define her three-dimensional body (Figure 26). The montage was made by superimposing a transparent computer plot onto photographic paper. Giorgini placed a transparent sheet with opaque lines on top of the photographic paper. The process was similar to the photogram process. He then exposed the emulsion paper simultaneously with a negative of the woman's picture.

Figure 25 (far left). *Surfaces: Folio* 3 (American Flag), 1976. Screen-print on paper, 20 x 26 in.

Figure 26 (immediate left). *Nude*, circa 1976. Photomontage, 12 x 16 in.

Giorgini's depiction of body contours using the computer demonstrates his ability to define form mathematically. His dark room experiments influenced his ideas for his installation. Instead of an inexpensive and less durable electrostatic print, Giorgini opted to produce his new work using a photographic process.

Giorgini started this process by bringing the electrostatic copies of his paintings to a photographic studio to make transparent negatives of his works. The new fully transparent negatives were ideal to create photograms, as opposed to the Mylar option, which was only semitransparent. Giorgini made different paintings in separate modules to create two massive computer art murals. The 126-by-84-inch piece entitled *Sculptural Forms* is comprised of nine separate modules; *Fiat Lux* is 144-by-87 inches in a single panel. The final pieces were created in a photo studio located in Indianapolis. Massimiliano recalled how his father took him and Flaviano on the "adventure" of picking up the final pieces in a rented box truck, driving about 70 miles south of Lafayette.[39] The framed works were installed at the Potter Center in June 1977 and remained on display until 2012. Figure 27 shows the design of *Fiat Lux* in a letter-size format photomontage.

For *Sculptural Forms* (Figure 28), Giorgini created sixteen image variations from a program named Light A. Giorgini created thirty-two different prototypes and chose nine for the final installation in the Potter Center. For *Fiat Lux*, he used the program Light B to create the initial composition of the mural. The design began as a seventy-one-by-forty-eight-inch Mylar painting that Giorgini used to prototype his composition on a smaller scale. After refining the light source intensities with his program, he divided the designed composition into six vertical fragments and printed them in thirty-six-inch-wide sections. The painted surfaces were transferred into a single piece of photographic paper using the photogram technique. Due to Giorgini's elaborate process, *Fiat Lux* is one of his most significant works. Viewers of the work perceive an optical and aesthetic experience while being physically immersed in the large-scale photogram. *Fiat Lux* constitutes a landmark in Giorgini's work not only for its complexity of form and technique, but also because it was the last of the *Surfaces* series.

The Last Stretch

The success of Giorgini's computer art during 1975 and 1978 contrasted with the death of his wife, Elena, in 1978 after a prolonged illness. Giorgini was left behind to take care of his two young boys. In the subsequent years, Giorgini's work evolved in a new direction, leaving behind the *Surfaces* theme (to be only briefly revisited in 1981 with a software called Stretch). The new program allowed Giorgini to manipulate vector primitives using his own mathematical model. Although manuscripts with the software Stretch were found at Giorgini's estate,[40] the intricate new stretched designs never became more than computer plots. Only a few unpainted lines were found, revealing an incomplete body of work (see Figures 29 and 30).

In 1979, Giorgini developed a new interest in a colorful and three-dimensional modeling software. This dominated his subsequent approach to computer art, as he moved away from the stretched surfaces and a new generation of Giorgini's creations began.

Figure 27. *Fiat Lux*, circa 1976. Photomontage, 8½ x 11 in.

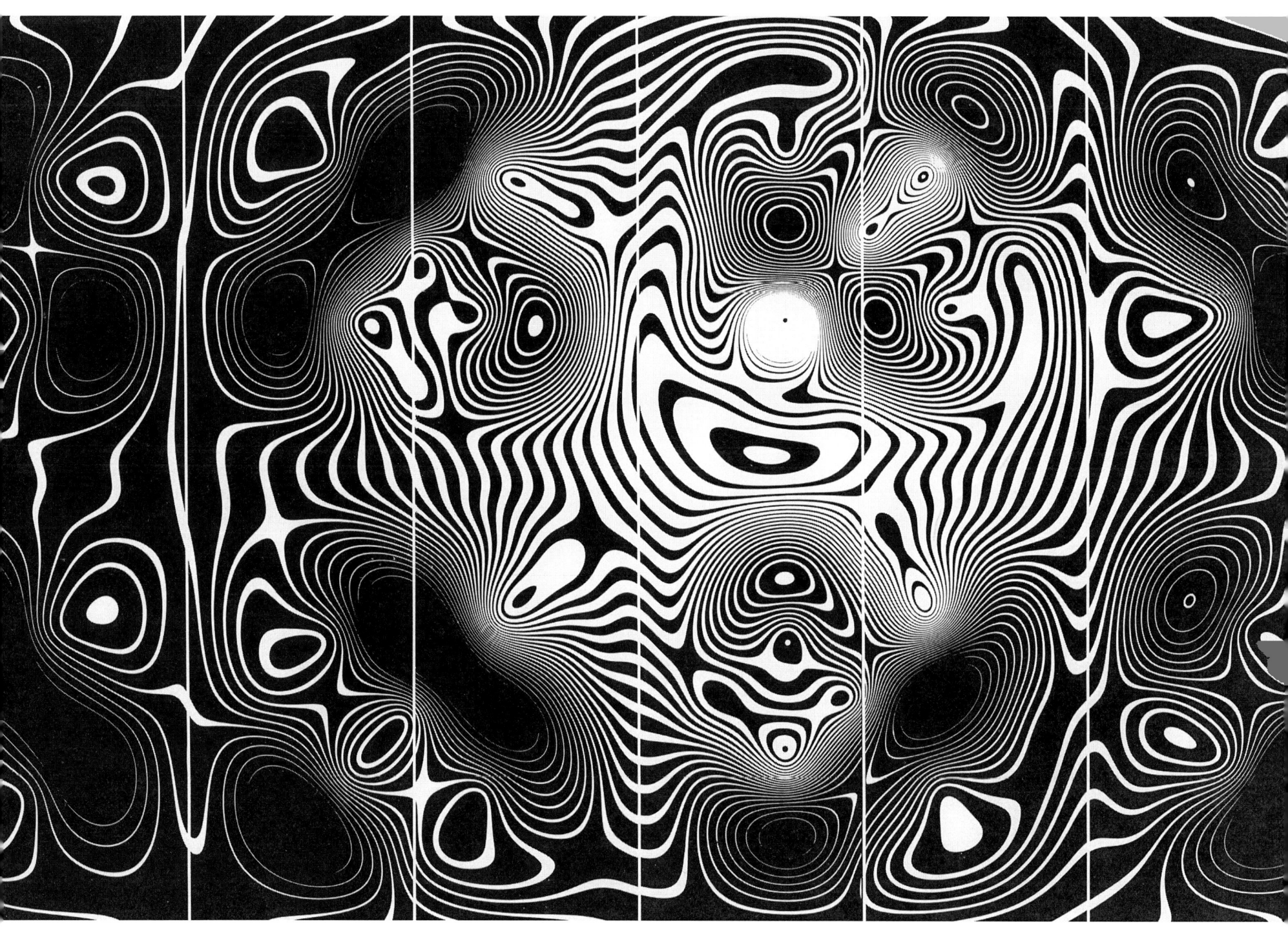

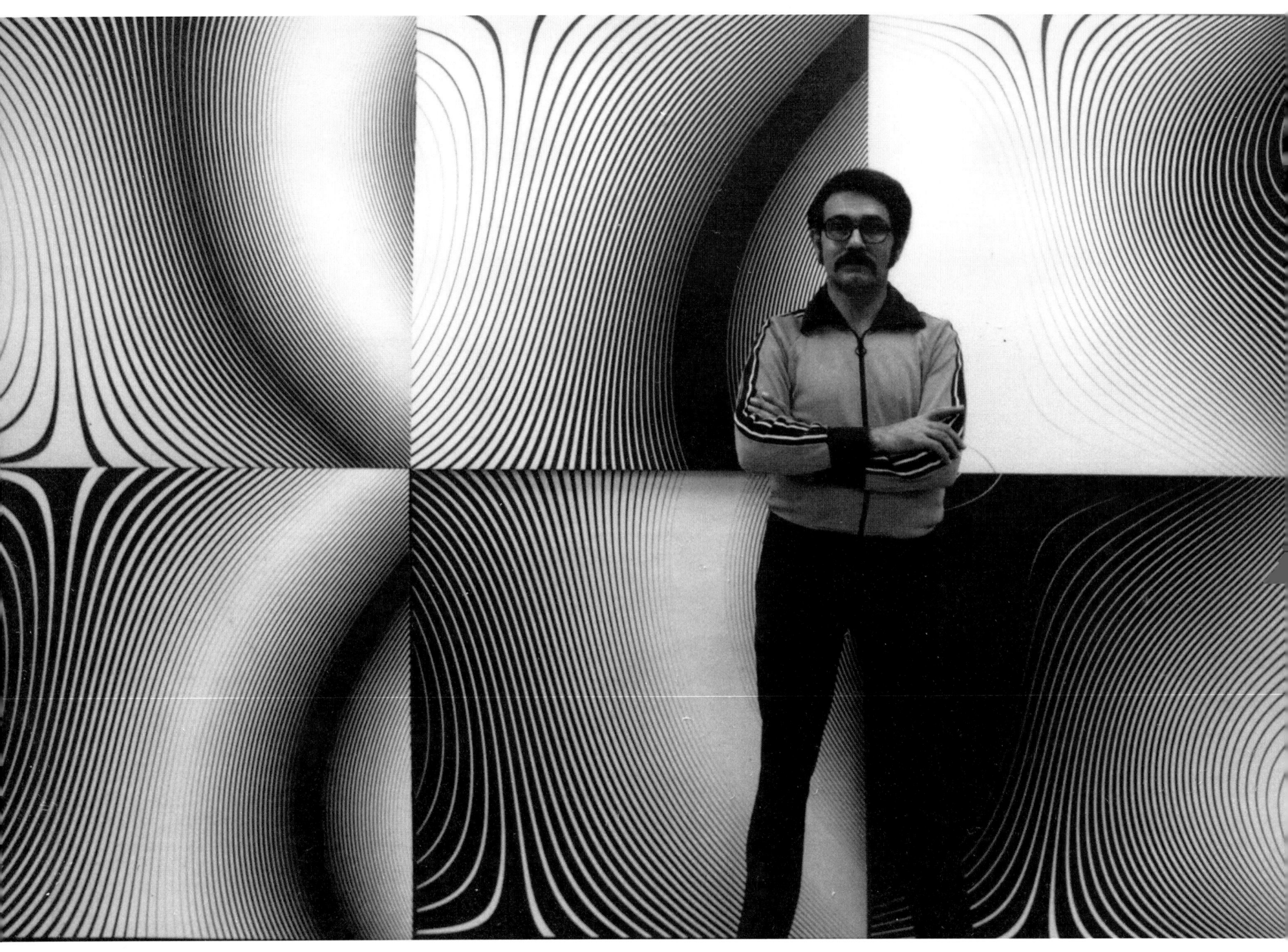

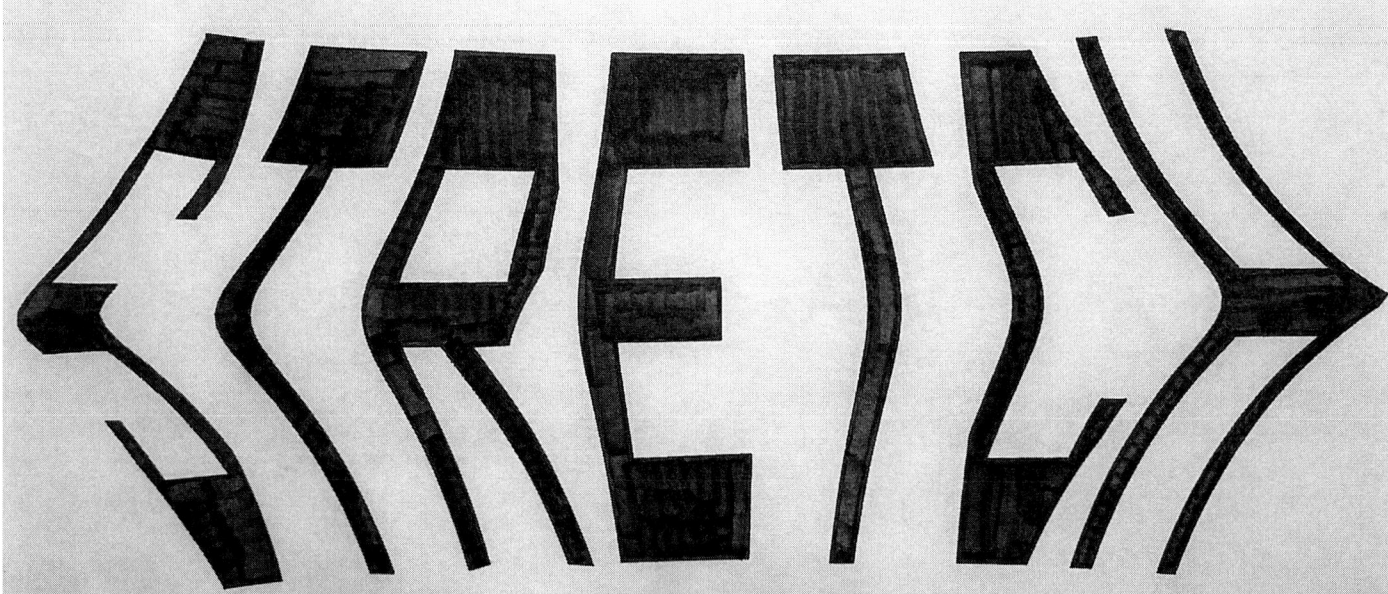

Figure 28 (left). Aldo posing next to *Sculptural Forms* at the A. A. Potter Engineering Center in 1977. Δ Photograph courtesy of Aldo Giorgini's estate.

Figure 29 (right). Stretched illustration for an unpublished 1981 report.

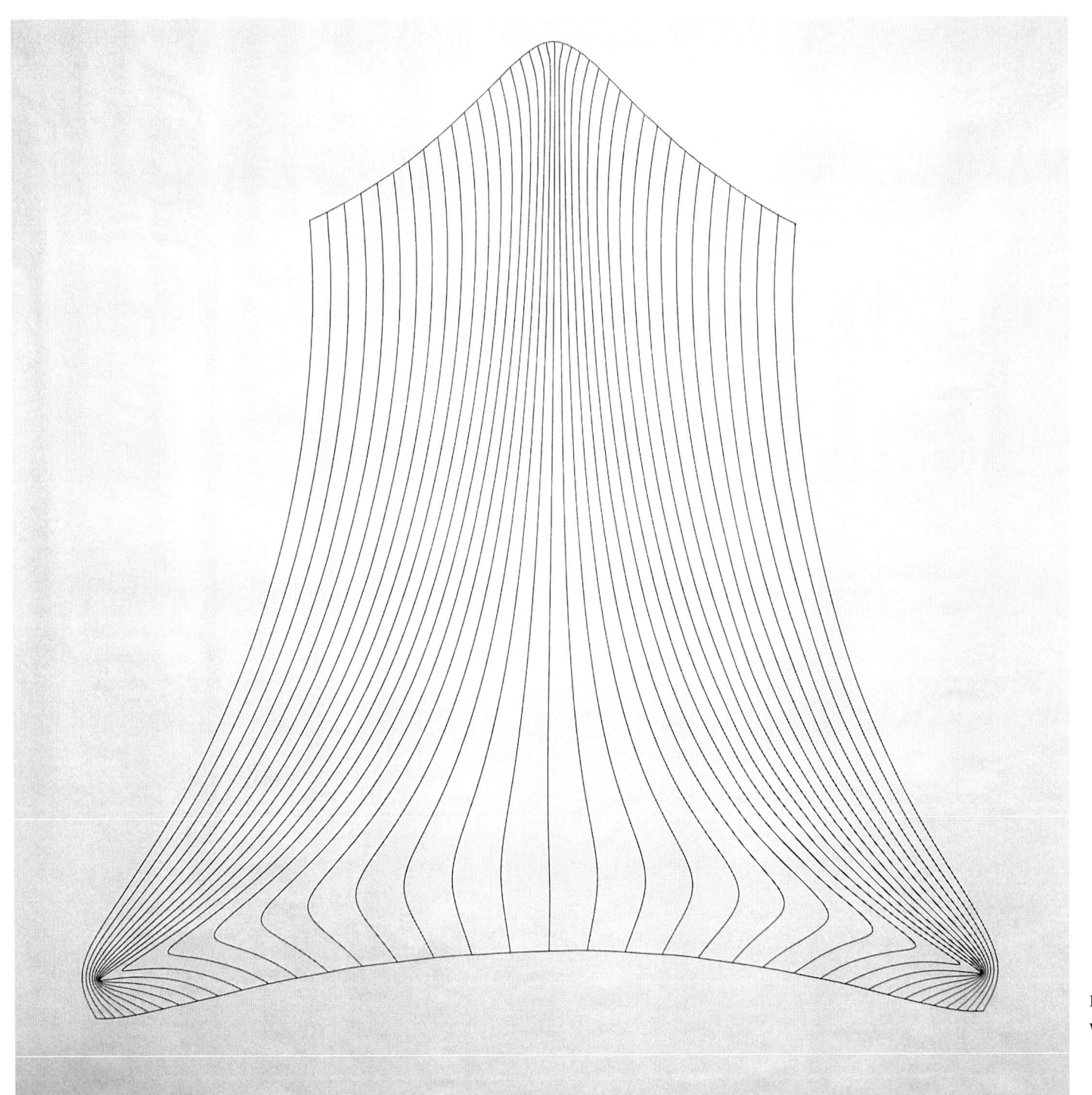

Figure 30. CalComp plot made with Stretch.

From 1980 to 1984, Giorgini experimented with Tektronix 4027A, an early raster-based computer graphics display. Giorgini complemented the Tektronix with his codes to render "quasi-photographic"[41] images.[42] Palettes and patterns with colors were superimposed in the surfaces of wireframe structures to produce abstract art. The resulting images took into account three-dimensional concepts such as perspective, value, and color (see Figure 31). In 1982, his work produced with Tektronix received an award from the German Computer Graphics and Computer Art Society. Recently, images and manuscripts that explain his innovative use of Tektronix to produce visual art resurfaced at Giorgini's estate in Lafayette, Indiana.

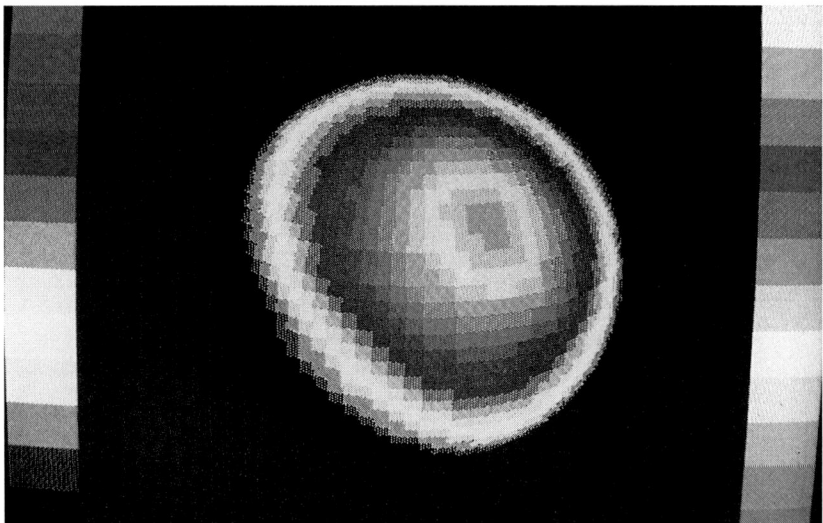

Figure 31. "Quasi-photographic" images were rendered with Giorgini's new programs. Note the palettes of values that define punctual light sources over geometry. 35 mm slide from 1982.

After spending five months conducting research at Giorgini's studio, I encountered a sheet with colorful Kodachrome slides. It contained untitled framed slides of three-dimensional visualizations of abstract worlds. Some of the images shared similar formal characteristics with Giorgini's earlier computer art, but these images had more visual depth. A month later, other materials found at his estate—including artist statements and color photographs of different formats and dimensions—revealed a new body of work subsequent to the stretched surfaces. Two new programs, Photo and Palette, provided Giorgini with computational frameworks to simulate the effects of light and perspective in geometrically modeled polygonal surfaces. An early raster display terminal called Tektronix 4027A, allowed Giorgini to produce colorful images using pixels instead of lines and paint.

Early Raster Graphic Technologies

During the late 1950s and early 1960s, researchers experimented by connecting cathode ray tube (CRT) monitors to computers to create visual output. Examples of these display developments include Sketchpad from the Massachusetts Institute of Technology and SAGE from the University of Illinois at Chicago. The initial use of these CRT monitors was to "draw" the image on the screen using vector graphics primitives, interpreting the instructions as points, lines, ellipses, or rectangles. The cathode ray would draw or project the image on the screen following paths, similar to how a pen plotter printer draws on paper. The image instructions were stored in a refresh buffer and redrawn thirty times per second. According to the computer graphics pioneer Andries van Dam, visualizing graphics in early vector graphics terminals was limited because of a combination of its prohibitive costs and simplified visual outputs: "Obviously, not many firms or schools could afford to purchase or lease one of these early refresh vector-graphics terminals. In addition to cost, the refresh display had another major disadvantage: The sketch on the screen had to be kept rather simple because the image would begin to flicker if too many drawing primitives were plotted."[43]

In April 1973, a new development took computer graphics into a completely different direction. Richard Shoup, a researcher at the Xerox Palo Alto Research Center (PARC), successfully stored frame buffers from a television monitor. Using a system called SuperPaint, Shoup and other collaborators at the computer science laboratory at PARC contributed to the furthering of imaging technologies. SuperPaint aimed to reach the following goals: "Making a digital frame buffer that operated at video rates and was fully compatible with video displays, cameras, recorders and other television technology, and finding ways for a human user to create and interact with full color 2D images and, later, animations."[44]

The program also played an important role in the development of the "desktop" metaphor for graphical user interface (GUI). More specifically, SuperPaint acted like a digital art studio, similar to modern-day image processing applications such as Adobe Photoshop. Based on the principle that pixels could be painted into different colors similar to a canvas, SuperPaint was capable of processing video inputs and combining them with computer-generated images. With time, the development of raster graphics facilitated the popularization of computing through the use of visual interfaces. GUIs that resembled personal desktops allowed nonprogrammers to use computers. Once displays became more popular during the 1980s, computer graphics emerged as the new discipline that we know today. The term *pixel* became popular as a unit of measurement for a digital image, as well as a unit that could store a location on the display and a given color. Paraphrasing van Dam,[45] raster-based monitors are a form of electronic pointillism.

It took many years for display terminals to become commercially available. In 1979, Tektronix introduced the 4027A, a display terminal that used a direct-view CRT, which allowed the graphics to stay visible until the user decided to erase the screen. Due to this, displays did not need the expensive refresh buffers anymore, allowing displays to become more affordable.[46]

Giorgini first became familiar with the world of pixels when he acquired the Tektronix 4027A. He developed the software art frameworks Photo and Palette for a raster-based display. These programs from 1980 show his approach to this technology. In contrast to SuperPaint, the programs that Giorgini created were instructions in the form of computer code instead of a friendly GUI. Something that may have encouraged Giorgini into acquiring Tektronix instead of another commercial display terminal is that the 4027A had the capability of reading Fortran, a computer language that Giorgini had been familiar with since 1972.

In a publication entitled "Interactive Display Techniques for the Tektronix 4027 Colour Terminal," William Gardner explains that the Tektronix 4027 color terminal had a resolution of 640-by-476 pixels represented in 80 columns and 34 rows.[47] The interface was divided in a split-screen manner showing two spaces, "Workspace" and "Monitor." The Workspace and Monitor windows could be adjusted to have more or less lines as well as a scrolling capability.[48] Giorgini typed Fortran instructions, visible through the Monitor window, and displayed the art compositions on the Workspace window.

The 80-by-34 spatial resolution of the image was small. To overcome this limitation, Giorgini documented his raster visualizations using color photography. The work was enlarged as big as 18-by-24 inches for display in art exhibits. Giorgini also created slide portfolios of his computer art, and he used to submit them to galleries and curators when they requested his work. Between 1980 and 1982, Giorgini produced new computer art while pursuing national and international exhibits and living in Lafayette, Indiana. Shows from this period are *Art In/Art Out: Computer-Aided Graphics* at the Ukrainian Institute of Modern Art in Chicago (Figure 32) and *Computer Art Exhibit and Festival* at the Lehigh University Art Galleries in Bethlehem, Pennsylvania (Figure 33). Both exhibitions also included relevant computer artists from the time, such as Lillian Schwartz, Vera Molnar, and Herbert Franke. Some exhibits presented all of Giorgini's work since 1974, but others only included more recently created art using the software for Tektronix 4027A. The new images made with Photo stood out from the rest of his earlier computer artwork, characterized by alternating black-and-white areas that produced moiré patterns. The Tektronix 4027A permitted Giorgini to include traditional painting concepts such as form, color, light, and perspective in his new computer art.

Bridgetunnel: *The Wireframe*

Giorgini created software frameworks for scientific or artistic simulations. A scientific background in physics and hydraulics allowed him to devise numerical models that could represent three-dimensional objects and spaces. While working with the Palette program in 1979, Giorgini produced *Bridgetunnel*,[49] a sequence of images that depicted navigation inside a virtual sculptural object. The object was seen by a virtual observer as if inside of it. The images display a one-point perspective of an object that surrounds the viewer and progresses toward the horizon. The *Bridgetunnel* series consists of fifty-six images, divided into five different sequences. With his civil engineering background, he was able to calculate forces and materials that allowed him to have a sculptural intent. To Giorgini, bridges represented the ultimate sculptural object: "We may be able to span the gap between sculpture and architecture and show that what we call sculpture and what we call architecture are but to extremes of a continuum, and that the bridge is something beyond this continuum."[50]

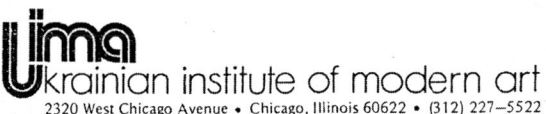

2320 West Chicago Avenue • Chicago, Illinois 60622 • (312) 227–5522

July 17, 1979

Aldo Giorgini
School of Civil Engineering
Purdue University
West Lafayette, Indiana 47907

Dear Fellow Computer Artist:

I have recently been asked to be guest-curator of a computer art exhibit at the Ukrainian Institute of Modern Art in Chicago to be held February 1 - March 16, 1980. The Institute was organized and is run by Ukrainian-Americans and is located in an ethnic Ukrainian area of the City of Chicago. However, they do not only exhibit art work done by persons of Ukrainian descent. I was approached by the Institute and asked to organize a show which will be entitled: "Art In/Art Out: Computer-Aided Graphics". What I am soliciting from you is your participation. I am asking my fellow computer image makers to consider showing one to three pieces of their work in conjunction with mine at the Institute. There has never been a major exhibit in the Chicago area of computer fine art. The Institute is frequented by the major art critics of the Chicago art scene. My strategy is to "blow them away" with as many works representative of our medium as possible.

This then is an initial request or call for participation in the first computer art exhibit in Chicago. I will be working closely with the Ukrainian Institute which has an excellent exhibition facility and gallery structure; your works will be well presented and can be priced for sale (30% gallery, 70% artist!) They have given to me the sole responsibility for the content of the exhibition. Please help me by indicating you will participate in what I expect to be a show that will illustrate the aesthetic magnitude of our technology-based medium. I will enclose an "intent of participation" form which I will ask you to return to me. Also if you have any questions about the exhibition you may write or call me or contact Kalina Pomenko at the Ukrainian Institute of Modern Art. Upon receipt of your favorable reply to participate, hopefully returned to me by October 1, 1979, further information will be sent to you.

Sincerely yours,

William J. Kolomyjec
560 Pacific Parkway, Lansing, Michigan 48910 Tel: (517) 372-2098

Figure 32. A letter from William Kolomyjec inviting Giorgini to participate in a computer art exhibit. Giorgini received letters similar to this one regularly.

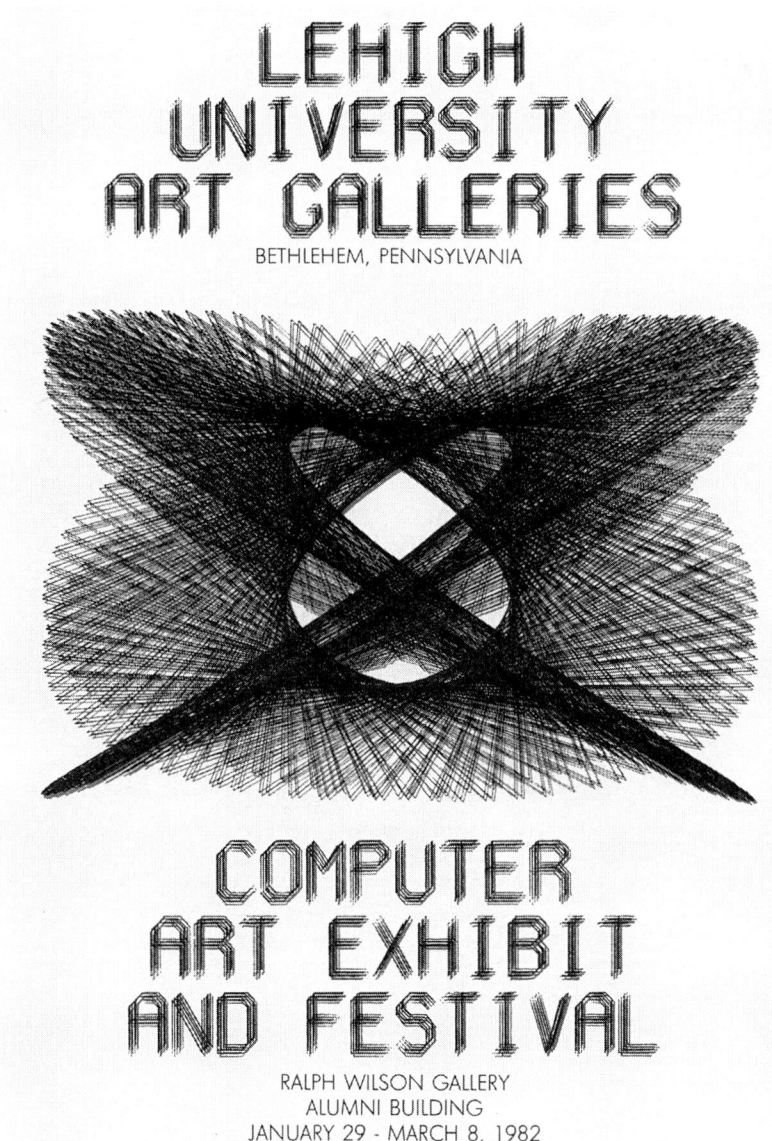

LEHIGH
UNIVERSITY
ART GALLERIES

BETHLEHEM, PENNSYLVANIA

COMPUTER
ART EXHIBIT
AND FESTIVAL

RALPH WILSON GALLERY
ALUMNI BUILDING
JANUARY 29 - MARCH 8, 1982

Figure 33. Brochure design for the exhibit in Bethlehem, Pennsylvania.

The *Bridgetunnel* images and a written record of his intentions were published in the 1979 American Society of Civil Engineers proceedings in a paper entitled "Bridges as Sculptures?"[51] The *Bridgetunnel* body of work demonstrated Giorgini's use of complex algorithms to produce three-dimensional forms and simulate the effects of perspective experienced by a virtual viewer. A visual example of this series can be seen in Figure 34. His *Bridgetunnel* series initially was created using similar techniques as his prior work with Fields and Surfaces, using CalComp plots with lines; however, *Bridgetunnel* marks the beginning of his new method for constructing depth mathematically, in a system that considered linear perspective and a viewer. While Giorgini was working on the *Bridgetunnel* plots, he acquired the Tektronix and quickly incorporated his three-dimensional models into the new raster-based terminal.

Palette: Creating a Color Space

The Tektronix 4027A allowed the user to change the color of a pixel by altering three variables: hue, lightness, and saturation (HLS). The HLS method was a newly created digital color model that became a standard in 1979 by the SIGGRAPH Graphics Standards Planning Committee.[52] The HLS system was used because it was more intuitive than the red, green, and blue (RGB) composition of pixels. Our visual-cognitive structure allows us to perceive the HLS color variations such as light, shadows, and brightness. The color range in the HLS method could be understood as a double-ended three-dimensional cone. Around the base of the double cone are the different hues, and the cone's opposing vertices have black and white. In this theoretical model, a color is represented by a point inside the two-sided cone.

Today, modern pixels can produce about seventeen million colors, but in the 1970s memory storage was limited; Tektronix could render only sixty-four colors.[53] Gardner explains that this was "not as limiting as one would first imagine as the range and number of simultaneously displayed colors can be enhanced via software."[54]

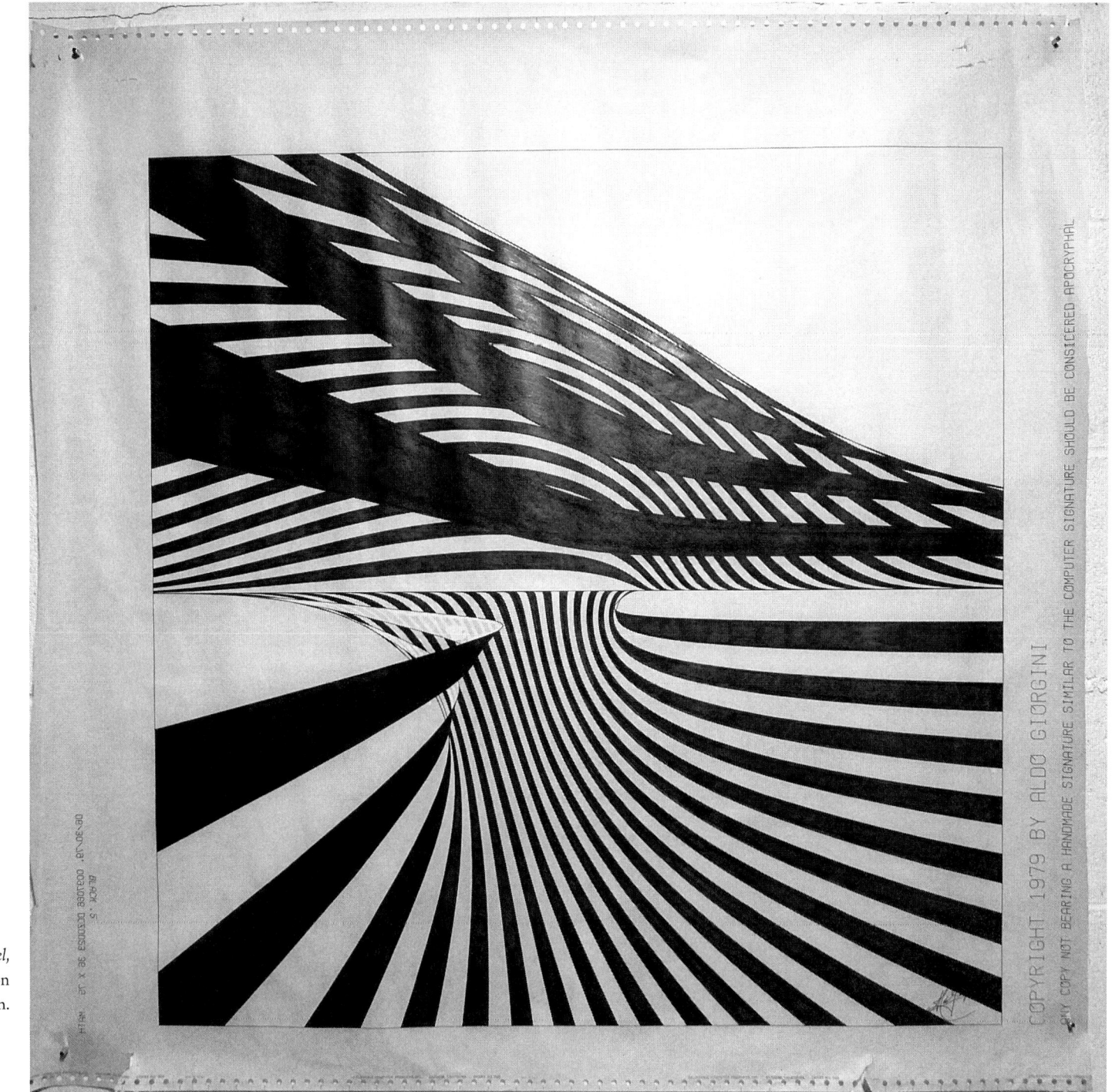

Figure 34. *Bridgetunnel*, 1979. Acrylic paint on CalComp plot, 37 x 36 in.

In addition to the pixel location, color palettes had to be created from databases of the HLS of each pixel. Giorgini's program Palette allowed him to create his own color schemes and patterns. The palettes were complemented with pixel-based patterns to produce textures and new colors. An unpublished manuscript from 1980 found at Giorgini's estate reveals his color creation process. According to Giorgini, Tektronix could display combinations of eight primary colors: white, red, green, blue, yellow, cyan, magenta, and black, stored in variables named C0 through C7. Each variable also could store an 8-by-14 pattern. Palette aided in the creation of new colors through the generation of seamless patterns: "It is possible to design patterns that would look like colors, once seen some distance from the screen. These patterns should possess the characteristic of looking as uniform as possible and, therefore, and as little pattern-like as possible."[55]

Based on combinations of interlocking color blocks, Giorgini was able to create a system to visualize 125 colors. Figure 35 shows the realization of this program as a visual output. Palette used a mathematical distribution to generate organized patterned color combinations in the 18-by-24-pixel Tektronix grid. The patterns could include two to four color combinations. Based on the amount of each color present in the 18-by-24 grid, a new color mix would be created. Giorgini's intent of making the patterns as uniform as possible was to create a seamless combinations that would cognitively produce a new color.

The combinations were created in an organized way to produce value variations. According to Giorgini, in an unpublished manuscript called *Palette: A Color Mixture System for Tektronix 4027*, "Each one of these color mixtures has a percentage of basic colors that can range from the scale of 0%, 25%, 50%, 75%, 100%."[56] The idea was to be able to create color gradations of similar values to simulate the illumination of a solid model. Giorgini was not only interested in making appealing color schemes, but also in creating a theoretical model that could be applied to produce the realistic rendering of three-dimensional objects.

Giorgini interpreted the double-ended cone model of HLS as a double hexagonal pyramid. Taking advantage of the Tektronix's eight-color system, his special pyramid had eight vertices. Each vertex represented the six "default" colors of Tektronix plus white and black on top and bottom (see Figure 36). The hexagonal pyramid proved a suitable model for visualizing shaded geometry. Each vertex of the pyramid represented the basic colors; hypothetical points inside the pyramid represented patterned shades of their combinations. Having an organized color system allowed Giorgini to create convincing value scales of a given color ranging from darks to lights. With Palette, Giorgini was able to simulate the value variations that result from the interaction of lights and surfaces. Giorgini first tested the mathematical models to mix acrylic paint and applied them to his sketches as a proof of concept. Figure 37, displays a perspective drawing of a checkerboard pattern shaded meticulously.

Cybernetic Landscapes

Bridgetunnel and Palette were Giorgini's initial steps to create what he called "quasi-photographic" images.[57] Giorgini's knowledge of wireframe modeling, perspective, light, and color allowed him to create pictorial representations of virtual landscapes:

In order to illustrate a three-dimensional object in photograph-like fashion it is first necessary to schematize the object. One such schematization is the approximation of the object to a polyhedron. In the case of an axis metric drop splash, the facets of the polyhedral surface are trapezes. This polyhedron is then

Figure 35. Palette's 125-color system, 1980. Δ Photograph courtesy of Aldo Giorgini's estate.

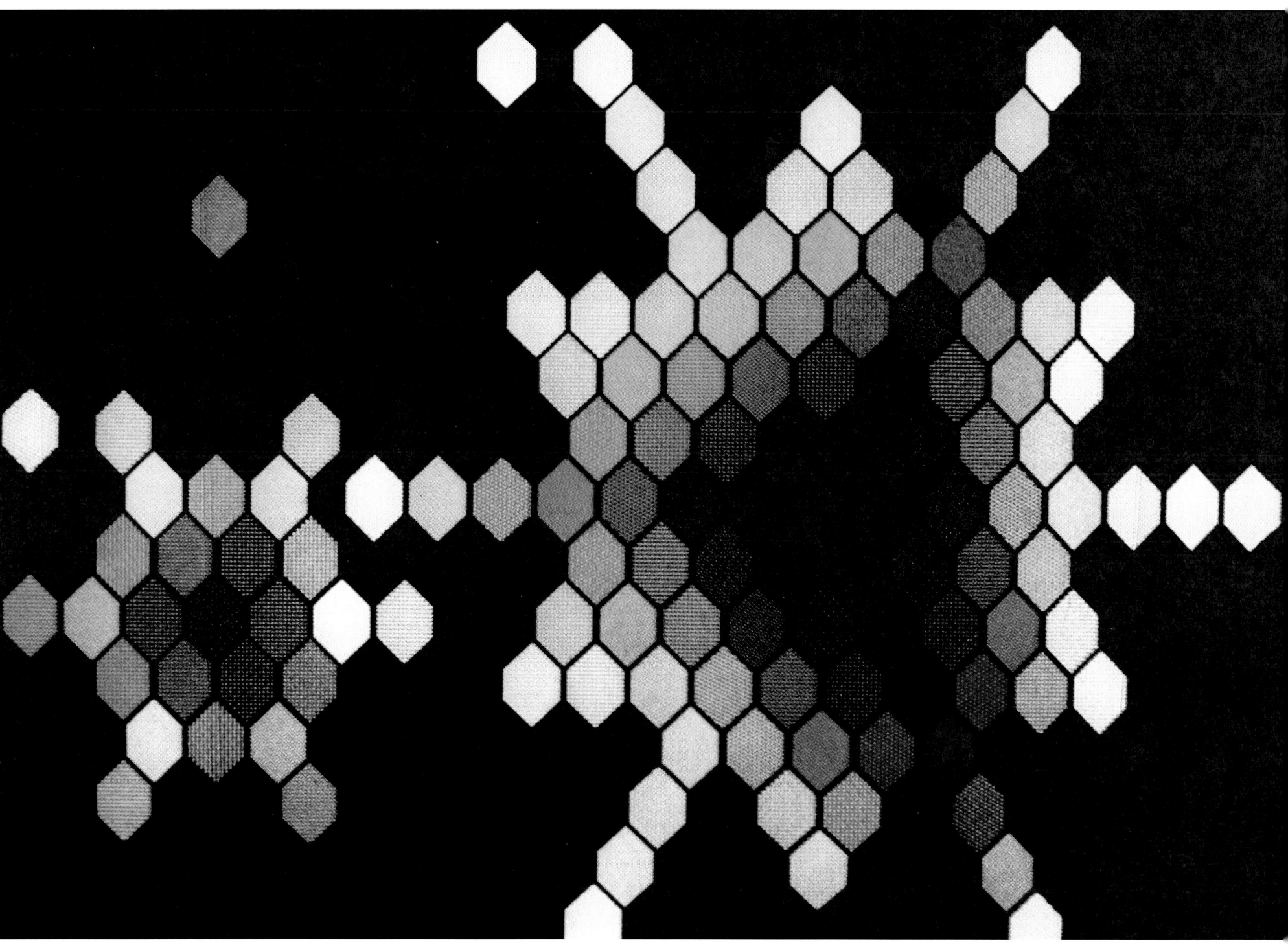

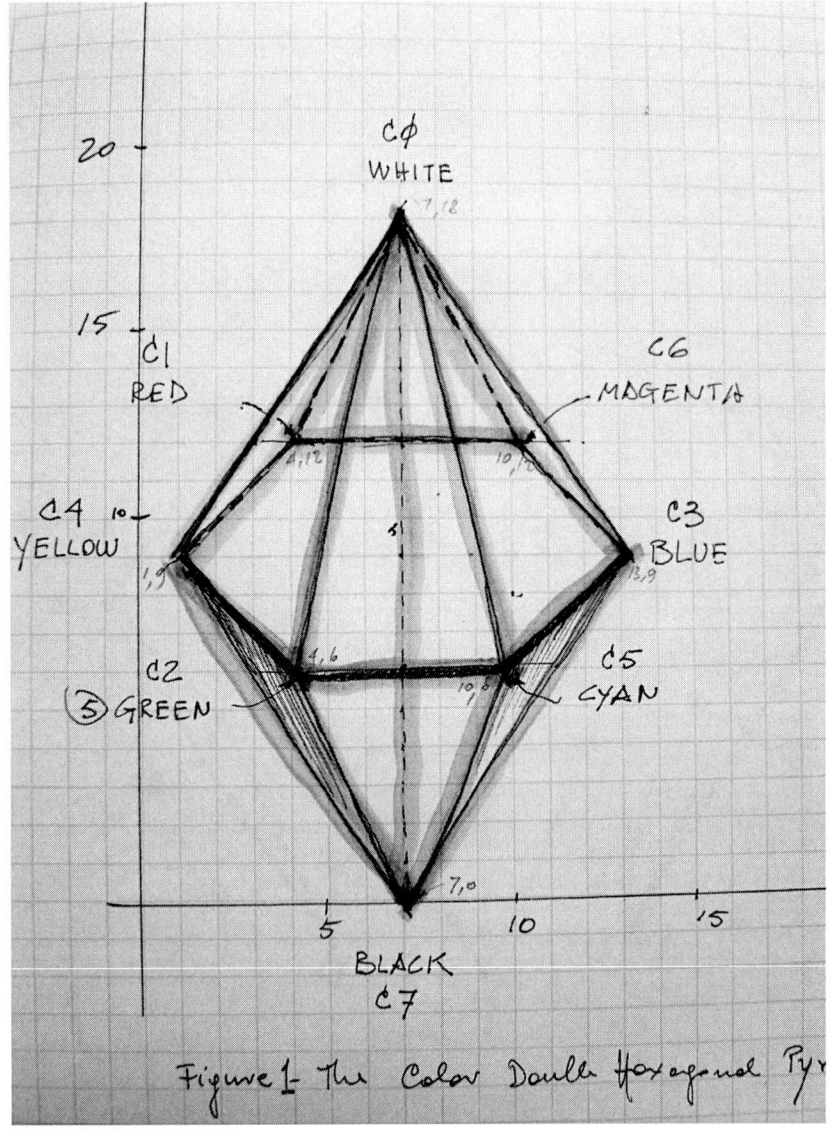

Figure 36. Hexagonal pyramid color model, 1980. Manuscript.

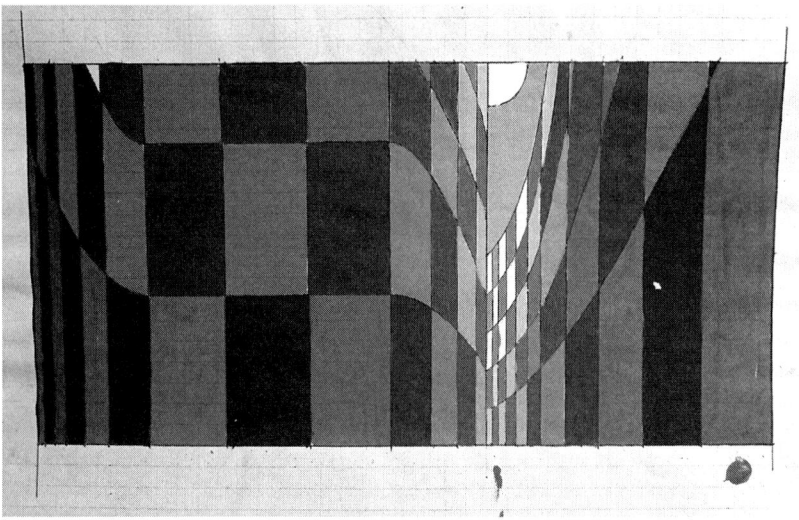

Figure 37. A painted sketch depicting the variation of color in a curved surface, circa 1980.

subjected to one or more light sources, is "observed", that is, it is projected on a plane called the picture plane, from a given observation point. The picture so obtained is colored with its colored attributes (depending on the color of the light sources and of the color of the surface of the object to be illustrated).[58]

A printed copy of the computer code of Photo from 1982 (see Figure 38), reveals the program's logical procedures within its commented lines. Two magnetic tapes stored the position and color of each pixel. Tape 1 stored the variables IXYZ with the three-dimensional locations, and Tape 2 stored the color of each pixel in the variables "IHLSA which contain[ed] Hue, Lightness, Saturation, and the reflectivity of each quadrilateral in the data base."[59]

The program also was able to render the images in three different modes: just lines, monochromatic, or 125 colors. The line mode, or MODE1, was used for the production of printed plots using a CalComp

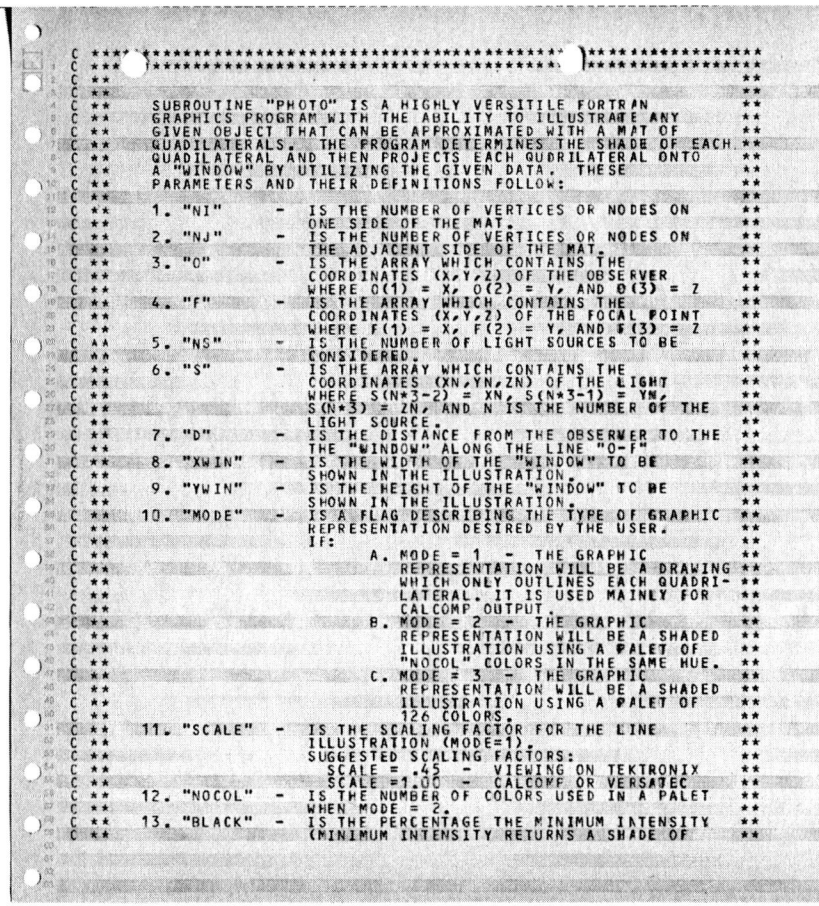

```
C ****************************************)**********************
C **                                                          **
C **   SUBROUTINE "PHOTO" IS A HIGHLY VERSITILE FORTRAN        **
C **   GRAPHICS PROGRAM WITH THE ABILITY TO ILLUSTRATE ANY     **
C **   GIVEN OBJECT THAT CAN BE APPROXIMATED WITH A MAT OF     **
C **   QUADILATERALS.  THE PROGRAM DETERMINES THE SHADE OF EACH **
C **   QUADILATERAL AND THEN PROJECTS EACH QUADRILATERAL ONTO  **
C **   A "WINDOW" BY UTILIZING THE GIVEN DATA.  THESE          **
C **   PARAMETERS AND THEIR DEFINITIONS FOLLOW:                **
C **                                                          **
C **   1. "NI"    -   IS THE NUMBER OF VERTICES OR NODES ON    **
C **                  ONE SIDE OF THE MAT.                     **
C **   2. "NJ"    -   IS THE NUMBER OF VERTICES OR NODES ON    **
C **                  THE ADJACENT SIDE OF THE MAT.            **
C **   3. "O"     -   IS THE ARRAY WHICH CONTAINS THE          **
C **                  COORDINATES (X,Y,Z) OF THE OBSERVER      **
C **                  WHERE O(1) = X, O(2) = Y, AND O(3) = Z   **
C **   4. "F"     -   IS THE ARRAY WHICH CONTAINS THE          **
C **                  COORDINATES (X,Y,Z) OF THE FOCAL POINT   **
C **                  WHERE F(1) = X, F(2) = Y, AND F(3) = Z   **
C **   5. "NS"    -   IS THE NUMBER OF LIGHT SOURCES TO BE     **
C **                  CONSIDERED.                              **
C **   6. "S"     -   IS THE ARRAY WHICH CONTAINS THE          **
C **                  COORDINATES (XN,YN,ZN) OF THE LIGHT      **
C **                  WHERE S(N*3-2) = XN, S(N*3-1) = YN,      **
C **                  S(N*3) = ZN, AND N IS THE NUMBER OF THE  **
C **                  LIGHT SOURCE.                            **
C **   7. "D"     -   IS THE DISTANCE FROM THE OBSERVER TO THE **
C **                  THE "WINDOW" ALONG THE LINE "O-F".       **
C **   8. "XWIN"  -   IS THE WIDTH OF THE "WINDOW" TO BE       **
C **                  SHOWN IN THE ILLUSTRATION.               **
C **   9. "YWIN"  -   IS THE HEIGHT OF THE "WINDOW" TO BE      **
C **                  SHOWN IN THE ILLUSTRATION.               **
C **   10. "MODE" -   IS A FLAG DESCRIBING THE TYPE OF GRAPHIC **
C **                  REPRESENTATION DESIRED BY THE USER.      **
C **                  IF:                                      **
C **                  A. MODE = 1  -  THE GRAPHIC              **
C **                     REPRESENTATION WILL BE A DRAWING      **
C **                     WHICH ONLY OUTLINES EACH QUADRI-      **
C **                     LATERAL. IT IS USED MAINLY FOR        **
C **                     CALCOMP OUTPUT.                       **
C **                  B. MODE = 2  -  THE GRAPHIC              **
C **                     REPRESENTATION WILL BE A SHADED       **
C **                     ILLUSTRATION USING A PALET OF         **
C **                     "NOCOL" COLORS IN THE SAME HUE.       **
C **                  C. MODE = 3  -  THE GRAPHIC              **
C **                     REPRESENTATION WILL BE A SHADED       **
C **                     ILLUSTRATION USING A PALET OF         **
C **                     126 COLORS.                           **
C **   11. "SCALE" -  IS THE SCALING FACTOR FOR THE LINE       **
C **                  ILLUSTRATION (MODE=1).                   **
C **                  SUGGESTED SCALING FACTORS:               **
C **                  SCALE =.45  -  VIEWING ON TEKTRONIX      **
C **                  SCALE =1.00 -  CALCOMP OR VERSATEC       **
C **   12. "NOCOL" -  IS THE NUMBER OF COLORS USED IN A PALET  **
C **                  WHEN MODE = 2.                           **
C **   13. "BLACK" -  IS THE PERCENTAGE THE MINIMUM INTENSITY  **
C **                  (MINIMUM INTENSITY RETURNS A SHADE OF    **
C **                                                          **
```

Figure 38. Photo manual, computer code from 1982.

plotter. Giorgini was only able to create visual documentations of the monochromatic MODE2 or the colorful MODE3 by photographing the Tektronix 4027A's screen.

Art statements written by Giorgini complemented the 1982 solo art exhibit of 18-by-24-inch enlargements of computer art photographs at the Northern Indiana Arts Association in Munster, Indiana. *Bridgetunnel, Canyon, Drop, Pearl, Saddle, Corten Steel, Pueblo,* and *Between Subject and Predicate,* developed during the winter of 1981, were exhibited in Munster and then internationally. The statements articulate his artistic intentions with the Photo software. During my investigation, I found twenty-eight photographic images on film and paper at Giorgini's studio. These materials reveal a variety of themes within Giorgini's art made with Photo. Most of the artworks depict aerial views of cybernetic landscapes with shapes of varied colors, textures, and illuminations. Other kinds of images were created by altering vertex points of three-dimensional solids using a stochastic process, a numerical model to simulate randomness.

Landscape Images

Giorgini deliberately decided to simulate land using algorithms. For example, *Canyon* consisted of a sequence of four images that simulated the Ohio River's stream bed near Kentucky's Six Mile Island State Nature Preserve. In other instances, the images depicted the fall of a drop over a liquid surface. In *Drop* (Figure 39), a ripple effect is perceived in a sequence of four moments of a simulated drop event. Some images— supported on Polaroid prints instead of slides—show Giorgini's experimentation with the different color palettes, showing variations of color and illumination using the same composition. The *Drop* series can show a bright blue or dark and cloudy red sky. *Drop*'s surfaces change with variations in illumination. Other examples of color and shape variations of one model can be seen in the *Pearl* series, depicting a spherical object in a folded plane (Figure 40).

Stochastic Images

Variations in appearance among similar images illustrate Giorgini's interest of visual experimentation through the manipulation of stochastic numerical variables. Since his three-dimensional models were based

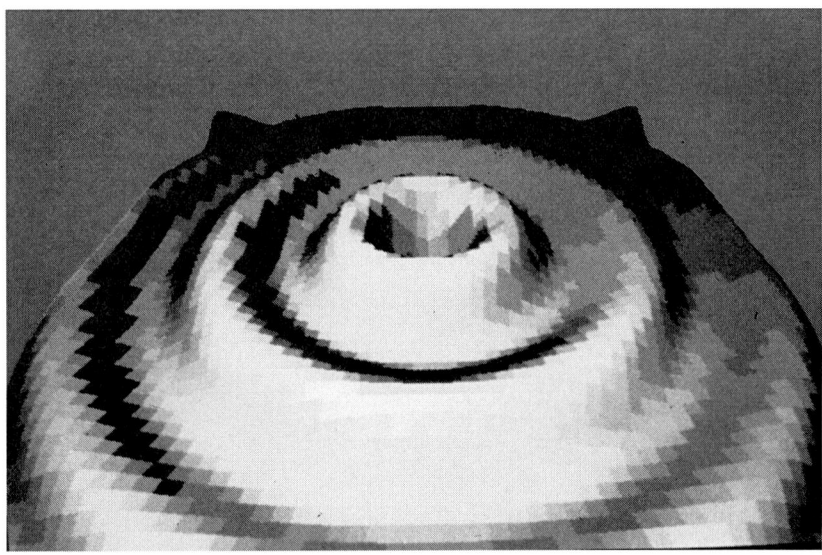

Figure 39. *Drop*, 1982. 35 mm Kodachrome slide.

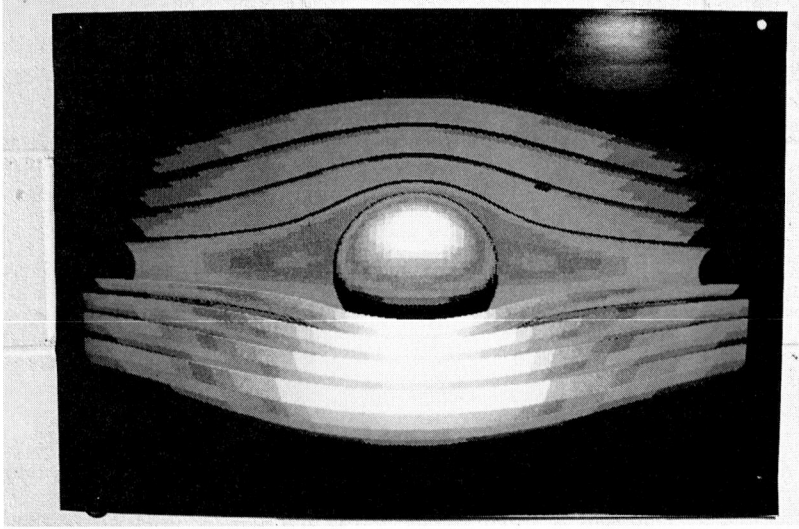

Figure 40. *Pearl*, 1982. Photograph, 30 x 20 in.

on points and polygons, he was able to reposition vertex points in the polygons to create new, unexpected compositions. By adding noise algorithms to his programs, he was able to create forms defined by a numerically simulated chance. A case in point is found in his work titled *Corten Steel* (Figure 41):

> The sculptural object presented in this work could be considered generated in the following fashion. A polyhedral object, composed of a large number of rectangular facets is represented in perspective view, under one source distribution of light. To this fundamental pattern a stochastic element is added: in the process of rendering the picture, at random, occasionally a vertex is not allowed to go to its proper perspective place, but is brought all the way to the frame of the picture. The result is therefore not entirely predictable, albeit its main features definitely are.[60]

The complex process of image creation was complemented with elements of play by experimenting with the parameters of the model's Fortran code itself. Sometimes the noise functions would reinterpret the geometry in an entirely unexpected direction. For example, in works such as *Pueblo* or *Corten Steel*, Giorgini redistributed the polygon's vertex points to random positions on the screen. *Corten Steel* is probably the most significant example of his stochastic work. In 1982, *Corten Steel* won first prize in a computer graphics contest organized by the German Computer Graphics and Computer Art Society, which included internationally renowned artists such as Herbert Franke and Manuel Barbadillo. The association was created in 1978 to foster experimentation with computers in the field of visual art.

After his artistic use of the Tektronix 4027A, Giorgini continued experimenting with it, but this time with a scientific intent. Other large photographic prints from 1983 show Giorgini's use of Tektronix for the

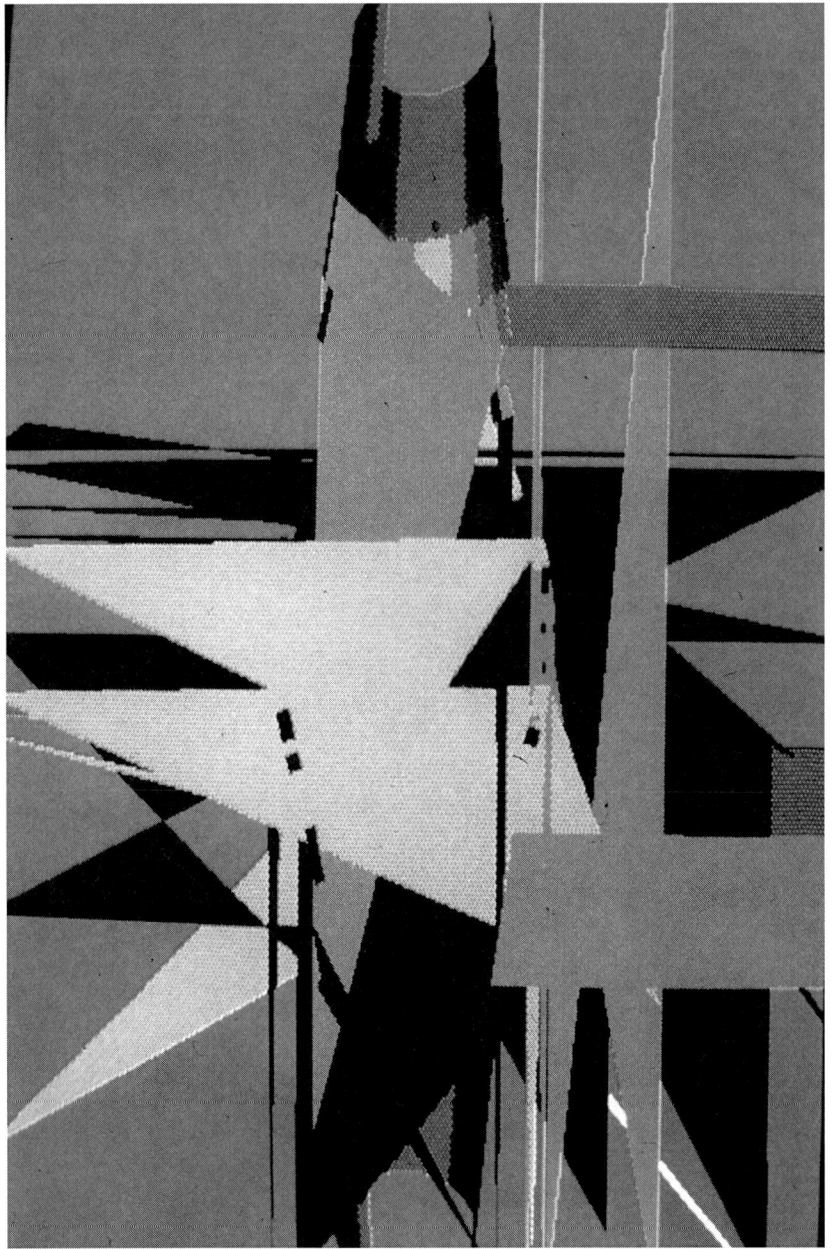

simulation of fluid turbulences. The scientific images that succeeded did not have Giorgini's artistic intent, and therefore are not examples of computer art. Giorgini's commitment to scientific research during the 1980s took over his computer art interests, which he had been pursuing since 1972. In the following years, Giorgini became an international luminary in the field of computer-aided visualization applied to hydraulics and did not produce new images or artistic software frameworks.

Producing images in Photo was a major breakthrough in the creation of more realistic computer images. Giorgini devised a sort of virtual world that simulated the effects of perspective as perceived by a human eye. Giorgini used computer graphics methods and technologies in the form of mathematical, theoretical, and geometric systems to produce early realistic raster-based renderings. His intent to develop this body of work from 1979 to 1982 was entirely artistic and constitutes the last example of Giorgini's approach to computer art. The results were new aesthetic forms: intriguing and colorful cybernetic lands.

Figure 41. *Corten Steel,* 1982. 35 mm Kodachrome slide.

During the 1980s, Giorgini transitioned from being a celebrity in computer art to one in computational hydromechanics. Giorgini continued to exhibit art, but more of his time was devoted to science. His developments in graphics granted him access to international elite researchers in fluid visualization. His expertise in the field of turbulence simulation was recognized by academics worldwide.

A sample of primary sources at Giorgini's estate, including correspondence, manuscripts, and images dated from 1981 to 1993, illuminate Giorgini's final years. The documents indicate three roles that Giorgini played simultaneously: researcher, artist, and father.

Researcher

Giorgini's accomplishments in computational simulation date back to his time at the National Center for Atmospheric Research, circa 1966. At Purdue, Giorgini documented his visualization studies in a series of 78 technical reports from 1968 to 1992, published by the School of Civil Engineering, with covers designed by Giorgini. Each technical report ranged from 60 to 200 pages, with a similar content structure: a description of the specific project, a description of a mathematical model, images, and computer code. Giorgini frequently would include the transcripts of the Fortran code used to make the images for each project. The scientific reports outnumbered those that presented computer art frameworks, which were only five: *Interfaces* (1975), *Surfaces* (1975), *Stretch* (1981), *Palette,* and *Photo*.

Giorgini's achievements in scientific visualization became highly regarded in 1981, when, in collaboration with other researchers at Purdue,

he helped settle an Indiana-Kentucky border dispute using computational methods. Employing the same technologies used in his art, Giorgini used the Tektronix 4027A and CalComp to create a simulation of the Ohio River bed circa 1792, when the state of Kentucky was created. A paper entitled "The Indiana-Kentucky Boundary Dispute: An Unorthodox Approach to River Hydraulics" explained that the boundary dilemma between the "trans-Ohioan" states of Indiana, Illinois, Kentucky, and Ohio dated back to the nineteenth century.[61] The Supreme Court ruled in 1980 that the boundaries between Ohio, Indiana, and Kentucky were the located at the "low-water mark of the river" in 1792.[62] "The problem was finding that level," Giorgini explained in a newspaper article.[63]

The team of researchers led by Giorgini used an innovative software called HEC-2, which was developed by the Hydrologic Engineering Center of the U.S. Army Corps of Engineers. The software package was described by Giorgini and others as a "sophisticated numerical laboratory that is used for computations in steady state open channel and river hydraulics."[64] Giorgini's team was able to provide scientific evidence of the low watermark of the Ohio River in 1792, taking into consideration variations in the water level and the gradual changes of the river's course throughout the centuries. The study was "unorthodox," as the title of the paper suggests, because it complemented historical records with computer visualization. In addition to HEC-2, Giorgini used his computer art framework, Photo, to simulate perspective views of the Six Mile Island (Figure 42), showing the Ohio River bed in a research publication.[65]

In 1981, the Apple Education Foundation awarded Giorgini $10,000 in hardware to develop a project called "Interactive Lectures in

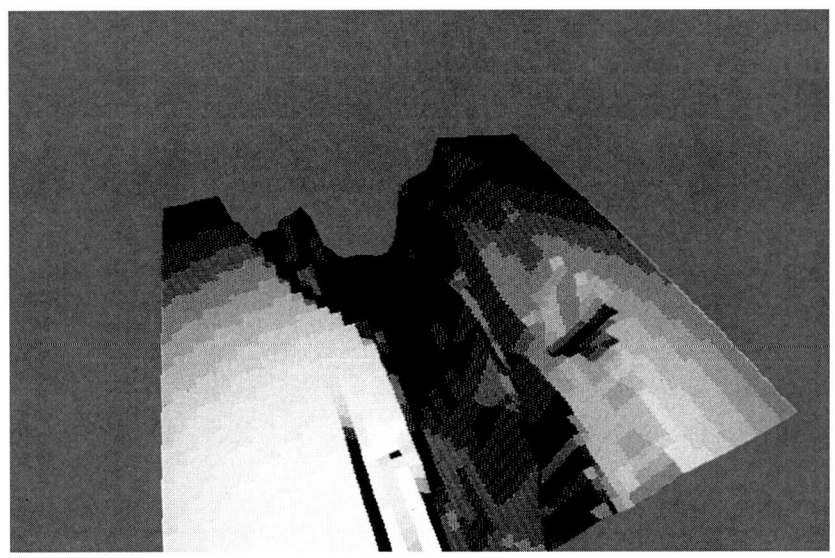

Figure 42. *Six-Mile island,* 1982. 35 mm Kodachrome slide. A simulation of the trans-Ohioan Valley.

also created teaching materials and textbooks for HEC-1 and HEC-2, helping expand the civil engineering curriculum.

Researchers visited Purdue from all over the world to learn HEC and other computational hydraulics methods from Giorgini. Giorgini also visited other institutions to teach workshops on HEC. Figure 43, for instance, shows a 1989 photograph of Giorgini surrounded by participants at one of his workshops in St. Louis. The image depicts a lab with several personal computers. The amount of knowledge required to use hydraulics software was often frustrating for students who wanted to learn programs quickly. A letter to Giorgini in 1988 from a student in Maryland stated: "As you are aware, my attendance at the short course on HEC-2 was my first exposure, but the scrambling to enter the data entry detracted from my absorbing all of the technical background that is

Hydraulics." For two years, Giorgini worked on creating Apple Hydraulics, a software for simulating fluids behavior for the Apple II microcomputer. This was Giorgini's first experience with diskettes and microcomputers; the project was completed in 1984.

In the early 1980s, computers were scarce and computation was expensive. According to a "statement of usage charges" from the Purdue University Computing Center (PUCC), the computational cost of Purdue's mainframe in 1984 was $28 per hour.[66] As the decade progressed, personal computers became increasingly common and affordable. The only limitation became whether the user had the proper training. Hydraulic software packages such as HEC and Apple Hydraulics required years of civil engineering education and familiarity with computer code. Giorgini taught separate semester-long courses at Purdue dedicated to HEC-1, HEC-2, and computer visualization. Starting in 1981, Giorgini

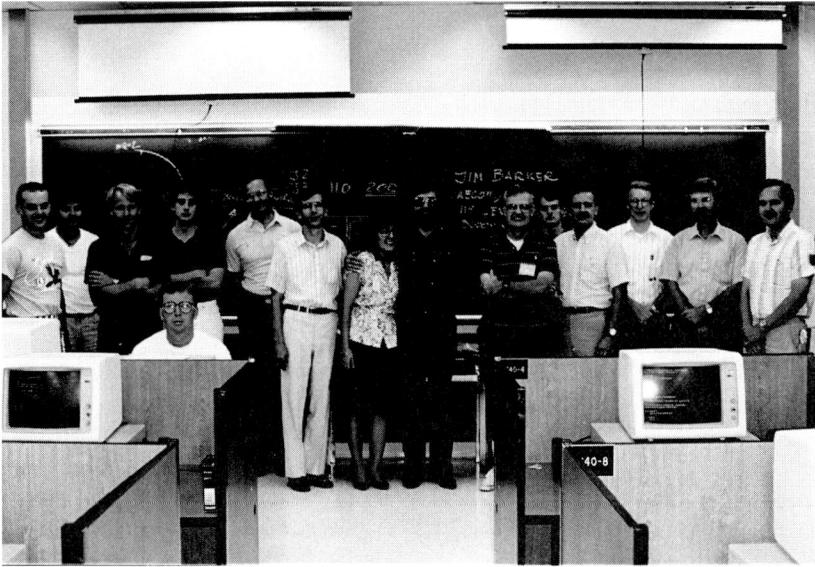

Figure 43. Giorgini teaching a HEC workshop in 1989.

needed to really be sure of myself. This is not a criticism but a statement of a fact. Imagine trying to do HEC-2 in twelve hours!"[67]

HEC-2 was a program made to perform complex calculations on river hydraulics. The output result of HEC-2 was raw numerical data. Giorgini used CalComp and Tektronix to create the visual outputs. His expertise in visualization methods, gained through his experimental and artistic use of computers, was also recognized among hydraulics specialists.

This period in Giorgini's life included a significant amount of travel. He became a knowledgeable resource for computational river hydraulics, and he traveled internationally on a regular basis, attending conferences and sharing his knowledge with others. In March 1988, he visited Morocco as an academic specialist at the Conference on Computer Methods and Water Resources. Later that year, he attended the Symposium of Refined Flow Modeling in Tokyo, Japan, to present two lectures on fluid visualization. During Purdue's summer recesses, Giorgini was frequently a visiting professor in his native Italy at the Politecnico di Torino in 1973, the Università di Padova in 1986, the Università degli studi di Pavia in 1987, and the Università degli studi di Trento in 1989. In his research he often collaborated with his graduate students, with whom he had friendly and long-lasting relationships. Based on correspondence he received from students and scholars alike, Giorgini was very liked and appreciated: "We are like your small brother, we like you very much," stated a group letter sent by his hydraulics students in 1993.[68]

Artist

In 1983, using Photo, Giorgini created *Vorticity*, a series of images existing between the scientific and artistic. *Vorticity* marks an important moment of transition at which his scientific research became increasingly prevalent. Colored fields are distributed to simulate the behavior of fluids around a cylinder. *Vorticity* is composed of four images, and an example can be seen in Figure 44. These images show that Giorgini's aesthetic interests are unquestionable. They are reminiscent of his complete oeuvre. One can observe similarities with other works, like *Negative Reflection* or *Light*, in which Giorgini simulated the interaction between cylinders and water. This research identified the *Vorticity* series as a turning point in Giorgini's interests. His foundation in painting and art provided him with the aesthetic sensibility to create images that could be interpreted scientifically. It became increasingly common for Giorgini to use new images in technical reports and journals, rather than displaying them in galleries. Giorgini continued to create computer visualizations similar to *Vorticity* for the rest of his academic career.

After Photo in 1982, Giorgini did not write new computer art frameworks, but instead, he exhibited his previously created works. Hundreds of pieces were found in his studio that were ready to ship and exhibit, made mostly during his prolific period from 1975-1979. In 1983, he exhibited at the Louisville Art Museum, and in 1984, he was invited to participate at a computer art exhibit at the University of Iowa. The pieces submitted were a linen transfer of *Negative Reflection* and the *Surfaces* print portfolio. Giorgini received an honorable mention for *Surfaces* at the Indianapolis Museum of Art in 1986, and they were added to its permanent collection. In the 1980s, other art institutions also added *Surfaces* to their collections, including the Carnegie Museum of Art, Lehigh University Art Galleries, Cleveland Museum of Art, the National Collection of Fine Arts of the Smithsonian, and the University Galleries at Ohio State, among others.

In 1986, he also produced a series of three posters with images from 1979's *Bridgetunnel*. The black-and-white posters were printed on glossy paper and retitled as *Landscape A* (Figure 45), *B*, and *C*. *Landscape A* also was used posthumously as the cover design for *Television City Dream*, a Screeching Weasel music album in 1998.

Figure 44. An example of the *Vorticity* series from 1983.

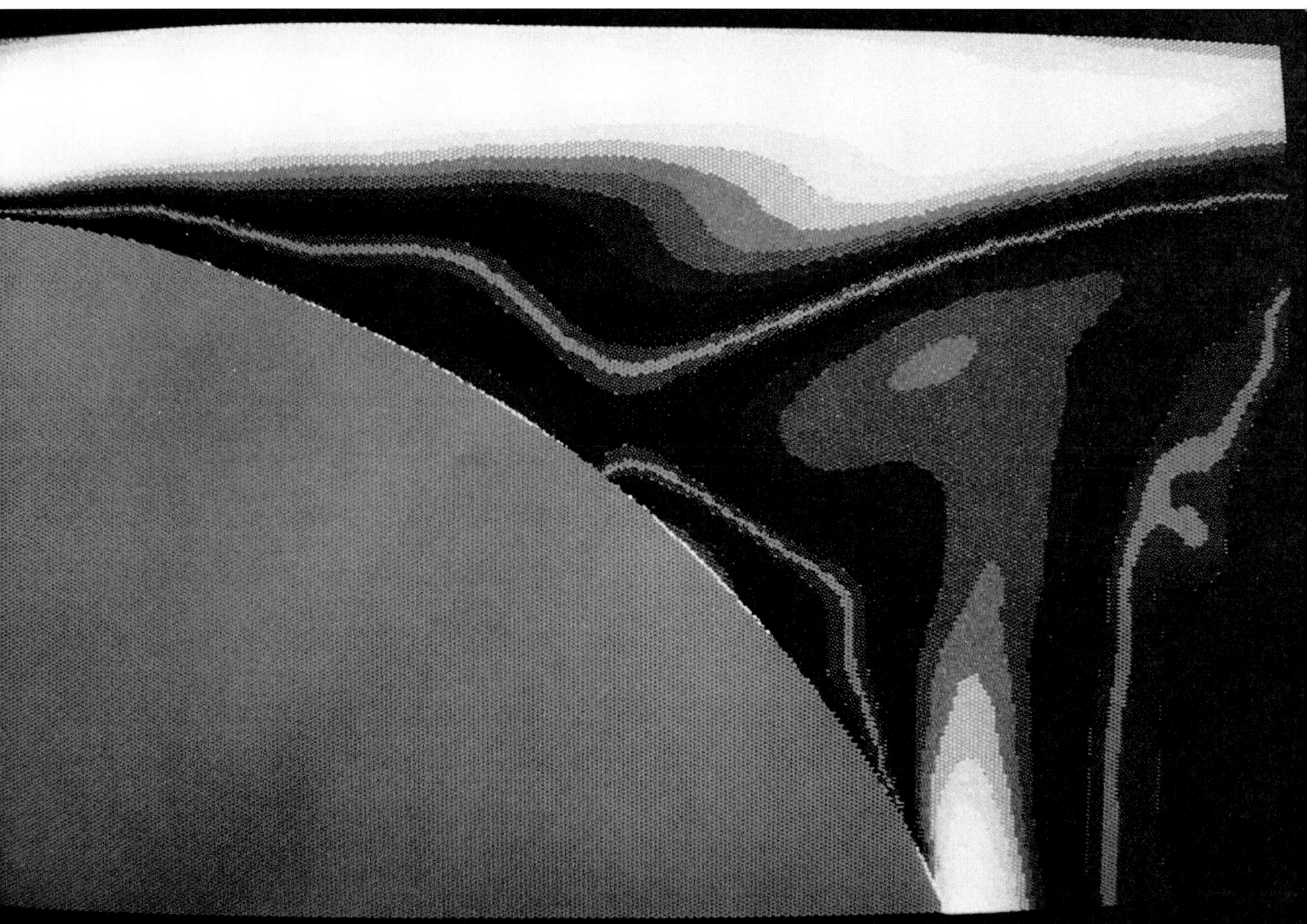

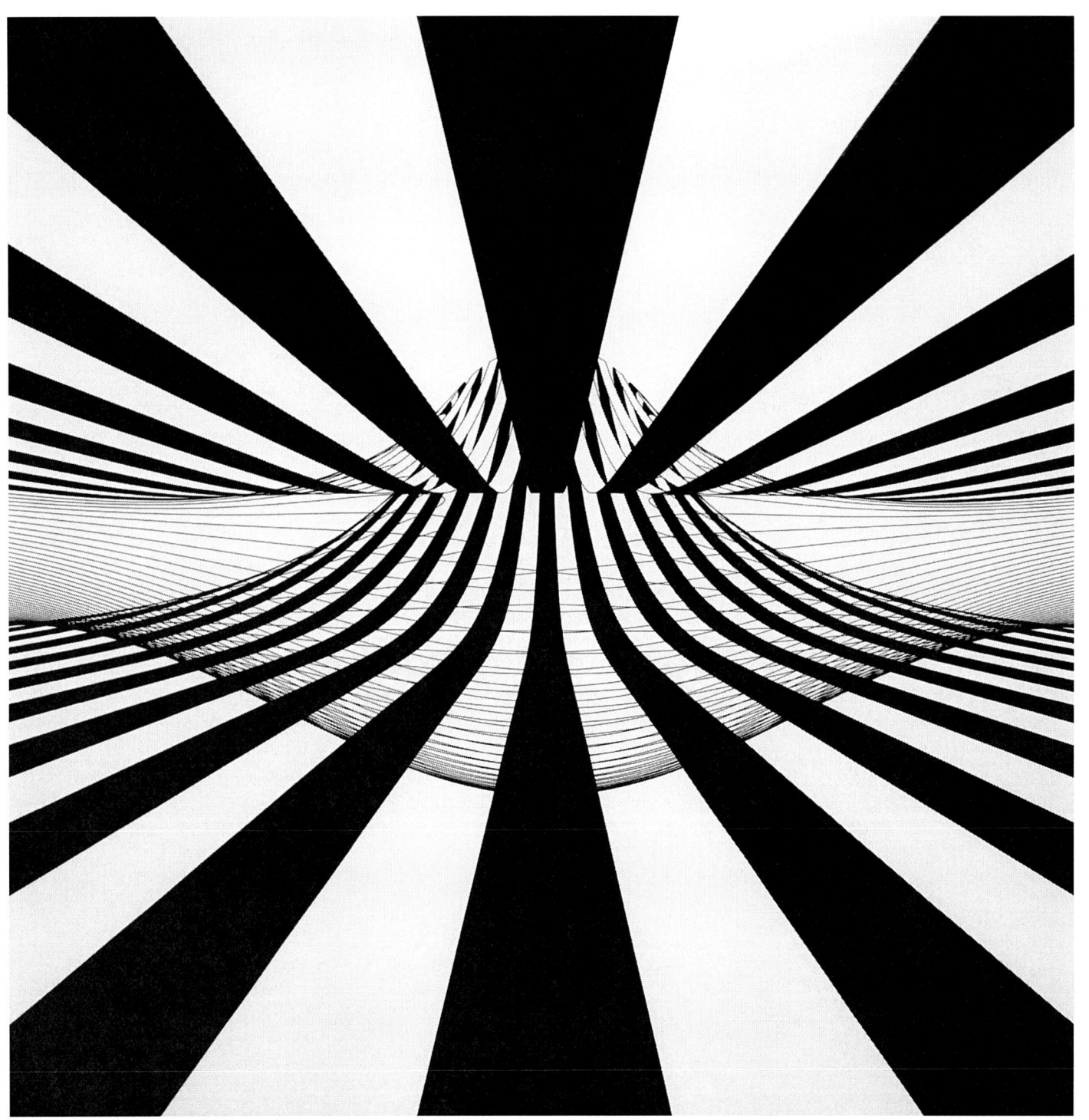

Figure 45. *Landscape A,* 1986. A limited edition poster that later became the design of a Screeching Weasel album in 1994.

The inclusion of Giorgini's computer art at fine art institutions during the 1980s parallels the gradual acceptance of technologically based practices in the art world. Early computer art faded away as personal computers became a more common art tool. Colette Bangert explained this technological transition in an interview: "Mainframes went away and we got our own personal computer. The expense went down and we could finally afford to buy our own little computers, PCs, and our own plotters. We didn't used to be able to do that. That changed everything, because you could use the computer on your own time, in your own studio, or house. That revolutionized who was called a computer artist."[69]

Personal computers fostered a new generation of artists, such as Margot Lovejoy and David Rokeby. Rokeby's seminal work of interactive art, entitled *Very Nervous System*, for example, was created at the artist's studio by playing with the tools that were commercially available at the time.[70] The new computers were affordable and didn't need a lot of programming knowledge. Compared to Giorgini's programs, like Apple Hydraulics or Photo, the new frameworks were not only easy to use through a GUI, but also could be easily distributed using floppy disks. Giorgini was well aware of this technological revolution. In his studio, he had an IBM and commercial digital painting programs, such as EGA Paint from 1986. However, Giorgini's art frameworks were more complex than the emerging software packages for art and design. Giorgini's programs were capable of processing large amounts of data to create three-dimensional, colorful, and time-based images compared to the painting-by-pixel approach in programs like EGA Paint or SuperPaint.

Giorgini had an exceptional combination of creativity and programming skills, resulting in his unique computer art. Other noncomputer artists saw his talents as an opportunity for furthering their work. However, Giorgini was opposed to a collaboration in which he would be just a technical intermediary between another artist and the computer: "I have found literally hundreds of people that would have been glad to collaborate with me. The formula was rather simple: Their ideas and my computer expertise. I have developed in time a technique of warding off such requests by simply stating the truth: I have more ideas than I have time to implement them. It seems that hundred [*sic*] of people would be thrilled to add the 10% of their inspiration to the 90% of my perspiration to come up with something real great!"[71]

As Giorgini jokingly stated, he had more ideas than time allowed. He was inundated with research projects and also a devoted father of two teenage boys. A widower since 1977, Giorgini had to play the role of both parents in his household.

Father

Giorgini was a full-time supporter of his sons' creative pursuits. Massimiliano and Flaviano were musically inclined, and while in high school, they formed a punk rock band called Rattail Grenadier. Giorgini provided them with space to practice, sharing his art studio with the band. Giorgini became a punk enthusiast himself, helping creatively with the band's image, on T-shirts and album covers. One of the most significant designs was for the self-titled album *Rattail Grenadier* from 1988, where he used computer-generated letters complementing a handmade grenade design. Giorgini became immersed in the emerging Lafayette punk scene, and he helped finance a live music venue on Main Street in downtown Lafayette.[72] The venue, called Spud Zero, allowed the Giorgini brothers to network with bands who visited from out of town (Figure 46). In a similar way that "Computer Art Day" from 1975 attracted significant computer artists to Indiana, Spud Zero featured acclaimed bands such as Naked Raygun or the Zero Boys.[73] Giorgini's strategy of networking through a local venue aided the later success of his sons, who today are internationally renowned musicians for their participation in the band Squirtgun. Giorgini's influence is also seen in the numerous flyers that he designed while the Spud Zero venue operated between 1987 and 1988.

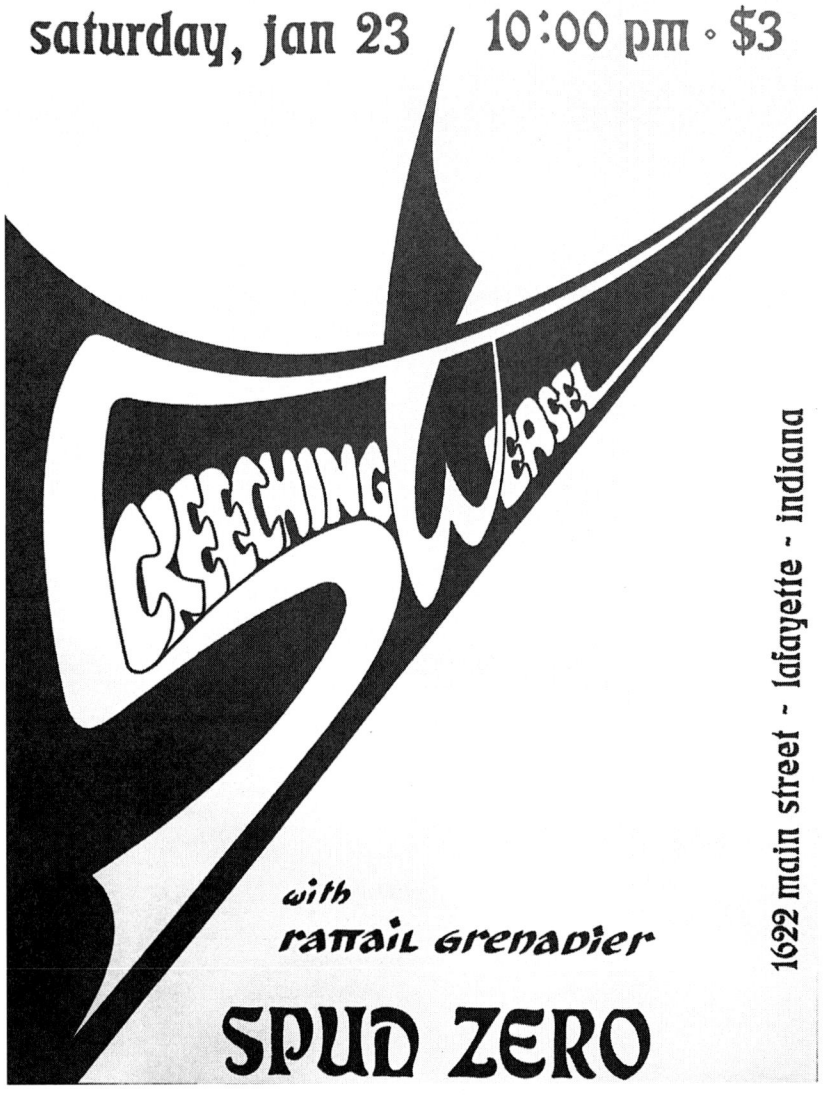

saturday, jan 23 / 10:00 pm · $3

SCREECHING WEASEL

with
rattail grenadier

SPUD ZERO

1622 main street · lafayette · indiana

Figure 46. Flyer design by Giorgini promoting a show at the Spud Zero venue.

Giorgini continued as a professor of hydromechanics at Purdue's School of Civil Engineering, leading a happy life surrounded by colleagues, students, and family. In the early 1990s, Giorgini started frequenting his native hometown of Voghera during the summers. He was planning to retire in Italy, in order to be near his mother, Pierina, and his brother, Giancarlo.

In January 1994, Giorgini became ill with brain cancer. His sons took the year off to care for their father.[74] Giorgini's health worsened and he passed away ten months later, on October 17, at a hospital in Indianapolis.

Giorgini was mourned by a diverse community of civil engineers, artists, musicians, and family. He left an indelible mark on those he met during his lifetime, who described him as warm and charismatic, with a special charm. He also made a significant impact on the history of computer visualization. Nearly twenty years after Giorgini's death, his discoveries still continue to be interpreted and cited worldwide.[75]

Giorgini's legacy lives on through his images and the methods with which he created them, continuing to inspire new generations of artists and scientists alike. As a researcher, he pursued creative ideas—new ways of creating meaningful images that could be read scientifically. As an artist, he was able to see scientific visualization as something more than just data. Giorgini's intricate optic compositions continue to inspire new generations many years after his death.

Notes

1. Massimiliano Giorgini, "Aldo Giorgini: 1934–1994," distributed at Aldo Giorgini's funeral.
2. In those days in Italy, the term *dottore* meant someone who had gone through a specific university program. In this sense, there are cultural discrepancies with the American attribution of the *doctor* title.
3. Massimiliano Giorgini, interview by author, April 5, 2013.
4. Giorgini, "Aldo Giorgini: 1934–1994."

5. Aldo Giorgini, *Aesthetics in Technology 1975,* from Giorgini estate, 10.

6. J. R. Travis and Aldo Giorgini, *Numerical Simulation of the Navier-Stokes Equations in Fourier Space* (Lafayette, IN: Hydromechanics Laboratory, Purdue University, 1975).

7. Aldo Giorgini and Wei-Chung Chen, "Interfaces, Computer Aided Art: The Program 'FIELDS'" (West Lafayette, IN: Purdue University, 1975), 2.

8. Giorgini and Chen, "Interfaces." Fragments of this report are included at the end of this book.

9. Ibid., 5.

10. Giorgini was a perfectionist. A mere smear of paint or unmatched pattern would cause him to start over on a painting that could already have had many hours of work invested.

11. Ibid., 48.

12. Ibid., 59.

13. Gerald Oster, "Moiré Patterns and Visual Hallucinations," *Psychedelic Review* 7 (1966): 39.

14. Ibid., 39.

15. Kit Basquin, interview by author, January 12, 2013.

16. Ibid.

17. Larry Bullock, "CE Prof Giorgini Connects Art, Science," *Journal and Courier,* March 14, 1974.

18. Aldo Giorgini, "Aldo Giorgini," in *Artist and Computer,* ed. Ruth Leavitt (New York: Creative Computing Press, 1976), 11.

19. Ibid., 6.

20. Aldo Giorgini, *Aesthetics in Technology 1975,* from Giorgini estate.

21. Ibid.

22. Roberta Smith, "Robert Mallary, 69, Junk Artist Behind the Growth of Sculpture," *New York Times,* February 15, 1997.

23. Colette Bangert, interview by author, September 4, 2011.

24. Ibid.

25. "Computer Art Day," *Journal and Courier,* March 22, 1975.

26. "'Computer Art Day' Scheduled for Purdue," *Exponent,* March 24, 1975.

27. Robert Mallary, *Computer Art Purdue,* 1975, tape recording.

28. Jackie Lipsky, "J. Lipsky to Aldo Giorgini," February 27, 1984, letter, from Giorgini estate.

29. Ruth Leavitt, ed., *Artist and Computer* (New York: Creative Computing Press, 1976).

30. Giorgini, *Aesthetics in Technology 1975.*

31. Lois Price, "Line, Shade & Shadow: Fabrication and Preservation of Architectural Drawings," paper presented at Brodsky Series for the Advancement of Architectural Drawings, Syracuse University (Syracuse, NY: October 2011), retrieved from http://surface.syr.edu/pres_brodsky/7.

32. Lloyd B. Walton, "Aldo the Artist, Former Computer Scientist," *Indianapolis Star Magazine,* May 8, 1977, 38.

33. *Sculptural Forms* and *Fiat Lux* also were titled *Light A* and *Light B,* respectively.

34. The photocopies made the brushstrokes look homogenized.

35. Walton, "Giorgini the Artist, Former Computer Scientist," 38.

36. Massimiliano Giorgini, personal communication with author, October 23, 2012.

37. Leavitt, *Artist and Computer,* 9.

38. Massimiliano Giorgini, personal communication with author, October 23, 2012.

39. Ibid.

40. The first chapter of *Stretch* is reproduced at the end of this book.

41. Giorgini coined the term "quasi-photographic" to describe his almost realistic visualization algorithms.

42. Aldo Giorgini, *Photo: Computer Code,* 1982, from Giorgini estate.

43. Andries van Dam, "Computer Graphics Comes of Age: An Interview with Andries van Dam," *Communications of the ACM* 27, no. 7 (1984): 646, http://dx.doi.org/10.1145/358105.358190.

44. Richard Shoup, "SuperPaint: An Early Frame Buffer Graphics System," *IEEE Annals of the History of Computing* 23, no. 2 (2001): 32, http://dx.doi.org/10.1109/85.929909.

45. van Dam, "Computer Graphics Comes of Age," 646.

46. Ibid.

47. William Gardner, "Interactive Display Techniques for the Tektronix 4027 Colour Terminal," *Displays* 2, no. 1 (1980): 45–55, http://dx.doi.org/10.1016/0141-9382(80)90194-8.

48. Ibid.

49. Aldo Giorgini, "Bridges as Sculptures?" Paper presented at the American Society of Civil Engineers, Atlanta, GA, 1979.

50. Ibid., 1.

51. Ibid.

52. Gardner, "Interactive Display Techniques for the Tektronix 4027 Colour Terminal," 2.

53. Ibid.

54. Ibid., 47.

55. Giorgini, *Palette: A Color Mixture System for Tektronix 4027,* 1980, from Giorgini estate, 3.

56. Ibid., 4.

57. Giorgini, *Photo: Computer Code.*

58. Giorgini, *Palette: A Color Mixture System for Tektronix 4027,* 1.

59. Giorgini, *Photo: Computer Code,* 3.

60. Aldo Giorgini, *Artist Statements,* 1982, from Giorgini estate, 1.

61. Aldo Giorgini, Dean Randall, and Andrea Rinaldo, "The Indiana-Kentucky Boundary Dispute: An Unorthodox Approach to River Hydraulics," *Proceedings of the Indiana Academy of Science,* USA, 1981.

62. Ibid., 259.

63. Christopher Reardon, "Purdue Prof Helped Solve River Fight," *Journal and Courier,* October 21, 1981.

64. Aldo Giorgini, Andrea Rinaldo, H. R. Lemmer, and A. R. Rao, "Graphec: A Graphic Laboratory for HEC2," Paper presented at the American Society of Civil Engineers, Las Vegas, NV, 1982, 3.

65. Ibid.

66. Purdue University Computing Center, "Statement of Usage Charges," 1984, from Giorgini estate.

67. Al Jungers, *Al Jungers to Aldo Giorgini,* January 28, 1988, from Giorgini estate.

68. CE 340 students, "CE 340 students to Aldo Giorgini," 1993, from Giorgini estate.

69. Colette Bangert, interview by author, September 4, 2011.

70. Douglas Cooper, "Very Nervous System," *Wired Magazine,* March 1995.

71. Aldo Giorgini, *Apple Hydraulics,* 1983, from Giorgini estate.

72. Massimiliano Giorgini, interview by author, April 5, 2013.

73. Mark Curnutte, "Club Plays High Energy Music: Spud Zero Fans Are Receptive to New Sounds," *Journal and Courier,* April 15, 1988.

74. Kit Basquin, interview by author, January 12, 2013.

75. Massimiliano Giorgini, interview by author, April 5, 2013.

II. COMPUTER ART IN CONTEXT

To understand Giorgini's contribution to the field of computer art, it is necessary to examine the historical context in which he produced his work. This chapter will outline a chronology of computer art, and illustrate the landscape in which an artistic movement unfolded (Figure 47). Rather than a comprehensive list of events and artists, it will explain the context in which computer art occurred, and the spirit and ideas that allowed it to happen.

What Is Computer Art?

Machines available in the 1960s were so different from the ones today that the term *computer* becomes difficult to define. Computers used in early visual experiments were called mainframe computers, which required the space of entire rooms. They were complicated machines that required a high level of expertise to operate and were very expensive, so they were common only in universities and research institutions. Since then, rapid evolution of information technology has caused the mainframe computer to turn into today's personal computers, mobile phones, music players, laptops, and so forth.

Computer art has been defined loosely as any type of art mediated by a computer. However, as digital arts historian Nicholas Lambert points out in his thesis, this definition of computer art can mean very little because the term can also mean *digital art*,[1] which incorrectly excludes all earlier manifestations prior to the digital age. Artists have been using computers for approximately sixty years, and it would be erroneous to classify all artwork produced (either aided or generated) by computers into one single category. Rather, computer art was a movement conceived by a group of visionaries with a common interest in using computers to make art during the 1960s and 1970s. These individuals were associated through a series of events such as symposia, conferences, and exhibitions, and they used the term computer art to describe their innovative practice. During this period, some artists learned computer languages and some scientists evolved into artists when exposed to the possibilities of computer graphics. It is important to mention here that the difference between a computer artist and a scientist lies in the artist's intentionality to explore aesthetic forms.

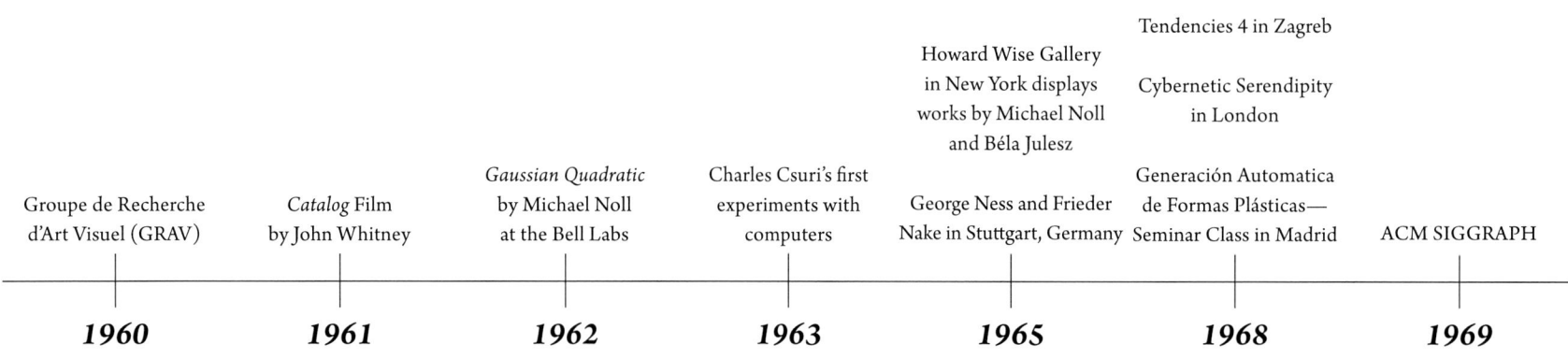

Figure 47. A visual timeline of the origins of computer art.

Origins of Computer Art in the United States

Early graphics developments, such as Sketchpad and GENESYS from the MIT Lincoln Laboratory, are important historical landmarks in the origins of computer-generated images. Computer animators Annabel Jankel and Rocky Morton[2] explain that the collaboration between artists and scientists was difficult in the early days of computing because neither side was able to fully understand what the other was doing. However, some of these interdisciplinary misunderstandings resulted in original discoveries for the visual arts.[3] For example, the artist Lynn Smith was creatively inspired after working for the first time with a computer, using the GENESYS software in 1969.[4] The original intention of Ronald Baecker, who created GENESYS, was to produce cartoon animations. However, Smith became intrigued with the visual artifacts unintentionally left on the screen producing trails of previous images due to the refresh rate. What seemed a hardware limitation to the computer scientist became part of the new visual language of the artist. Smith was then able to create abstract films using her discovery of this unconventional technique. Smith's work with the GENESYS software highlights a common theme in computer art. During the 1950s, the use of computers for art, industry, or entertainment was not taken seriously because of the programming effort required and the hardware limitations of the machines during this period. The "misuse" of new technologies for artistic production was a defining characteristic of computer art since its very origins.

Michael Noll had a similar experience with an accidental computer art creation. In his article entitled "The Beginnings of Computer Art in the United States: A Memoir,"[5] Noll revisits his early computer art experiments from 1962 to 1971 at the Bell Laboratories. Trained as an engineer, but with a sensibility toward art, Noll used the latest technology from that period to produce plots as art pieces. In the article he explains that his first experiment in 1962 was inspired from a computer error that produced an image that resembled abstract art. The result of this was *Gaussian Quadratic,* a print resulting from a computer program that operated under the constraints of random and defined angles.

Optic Art Overlaps

Noll also experimented with computer instructions to recreate art pieces by the geometric abstractionist painter Piet Mondrian and optic artist Bridget Riley. Geometric abstraction and "op art" were popular art forms at the time and shared stylistic similarities with those images generated by the computer. Op artists were interested in researching the visual-perceptual system. In op art, artists exploited the Gestalt principles to make patterned images and repetitions that produced vibrations and experiences in the viewer's mind. Examples of this influence can be seen in the meticulous paintings of Victor Vasarely, Carlos Cruz-Diez, and François Morellet, who belonged to an international group of artists called Groupe de Recherche d'Art Visuel (GRAV).[6] GRAV was a Paris-based collective that grouped European and Latin American artists who were interested in the perceptual effects of color, composition, and geometry. Early computer artists and perceptual artists shared ideas about art as a field of research through the international movement known as New Tendencies, which took place from 1961 to 1972. One early example of experimental research in the fine arts is present in the ideas Morellet. In the catalog for the 1962 exhibition titled *L'Instabilité* at La Maison des Beaux Arts in Paris, Morellet explained the relationship between art, program, and research: "This programmed experimental paintings meet the great need for new materials for aestheticians, those scientists who are at once mathematicians and psychologists who, starting out from theories of modern psychology (in particular on the transmission of messages), are laying the foundations for a new science of art."[7]

Op art and GRAV did not use computers, but had similar aesthetic grounds in algorithmic form. For example, Morellet's work from 1958, titled *8 Trames 0° 22°5 45° 67°5 90° 112°5 135°*, consists of a series of parallel pencil lines drawn on the wall with increments of 22.5°. The resulting image is a dazzling optical illusion accomplished by the programmatic nature of the piece.

Op art and GRAV greatly influenced the origins of computer art. A case in point is the work *Ninety Parallel Sinusoids With Linearly Increasing Period*, created by Michael Noll in 1962. This work was created to be a computer reconstruction of Bridget Riley's op art painting, *Current*.

Another computer artist from the Bell Laboratories is Kenneth Knowlton, who, in collaboration with Leon D. Harmon, produced *Mural* in 1966. *Mural* is part of a series of "computer nudes" that Knowlton and Harmon created with early scanning technologies using photographic images as the source. The image was digitized using a special camera that quantized the electric signals into numeric data. The resulting image was divided into patterns of different visual density, producing gradual change of value. The picture elements consisted of combinations of computer characters, such as commas, division signs, and slashes, which made a representation of the original values of the input image.[8]

In 1963, Charles Csuri became fascinated with computers at the Ohio State University (OSU). Originally a painter, Csuri used a computer as means to manipulate images and envisioned the future of art by extending the visual vocabulary beyond the confines of traditional media. Csuri's first experiments using an analog computer were visual reinterpretations of fine arts masters, such as Albrecht Dürer, Leonardo da Vinci, Jean-Auguste-Dominique Ingres, Francisco de Goya, and Pablo Picasso, among others. At OSU, Csuri and Jack Mitten, a professor of industrial engineering, discussed the potential role of computers in aesthetics. It took almost ten years for Csuri to fully embrace technology in his art. As Jean Dominici DeMaria explains in her dissertation on Csuri, "Suddenly he was inspired with the realization that an output device could be attached to a computer, and the potential implications of that idea resulted in his decision to make his commitment to computers in art."[9]

By 1966, Csuri had learned the computer languages of the time and was able to experiment using film and plots as means of artistic expression. His early films, such as *Humming Bird* (1966) and *Aging Process* (1967), and the print *Sine Curve Man* (1967), positioned Csuri as an international pioneer in computer art. His role in the development of computer art, three-dimensional visualization, and computer animation is crucial in the development of computer graphics as a whole. Csuri's lifelong commitment to art education at OSU allowed him to develop an academic curriculum for this emerging art form.[10] Most recently, he was a recipient of the 2011 Association for Computer Machinery-Special Interest Group on Graphics (ACM SIGGRAPH) award for a lifetime achievement in digital art.[11]

Resistance to Computers in Art

Csuri's acclaim today is in contrast with the general skepticism of computer artists at an earlier time. Other traditional artists did not understand the intent of computer artists. Csuri "had to come to terms early with a considerable amount of misunderstanding and a certain sense of alienation from other artists in his department."[12] Another example of the difficulties that computer artists had are explained in Noll's memoirs, when attempting to copyright *Gaussian Quadratic* in 1965: "At first they refused since a machine had generated the work. I explained that a human being had written the program that incorporated randomness and order. They again refused to register the work, stating that randomness was not acceptable. I finally explained that although the numbers generated by the program appeared 'random' to humans, the algorithm generating them was perfectly mathematical and not random at all. The copyright was finally accepted."[13]

This interdisciplinary crossover between art and computers made some gallery dealers and artists feel "threatened by the fact that one could do art by pushing a button."[14] However, making art that was aided by a computer was much more than just pushing a button. Computer artists Jeff and Colette Bangert pointed out in the early 1970s "that pushing a button and doing the same things is pretty boring." [15] As a result, computer artists of the time sought to find spaces for this nontraditional artistic expression. There was spontaneous interest to share the visual result of these experiments in a public forum. One of the first attempts to organize a computer art exhibition occurred in 1965 at the Howard Wise Gallery in New York. The gallery showcased artworks from Michael Noll and Bela Julesz made at Bell Laboratories.

The 1978 exhibitions *Tendencies 4* in Zagreb and *Cybernetic Serendipity* in London validated this emerging art form. German computer artists Frieder Nake and Georg Nees presented the result of their visual experiments along with their American counterparts, Noll, Knowlton, and Csuri, during *Tendencies 4*.[16] In *Cybernetic Serendipity*, curator Jasia Reichardt gathered a group who made computer-generated pieces, cybernetic devices, robots, and painting machines. This show displayed films by Knowlton and John Whitney Sr., as well as prints by Csuri and Noll.

Subsequent to the international visibility of computer art among their creators, a series of independently organized events began to occur in the form of symposia, conferences, and exhibitions. The practitioners of computer art were interested in creating alternative venues to discuss and share their experiences with computers and to further the development of this discipline. One early network was formed through the ACM SIGGRAPH newsletter, which began in 1966.[17] The newsletter eventually evolved into today's SIGGRAPH conference. By 1975, it was common for computer artists to publish the results of their visual experiments in the format of a scientific paper. Examples of these publications are "Computer Animation" in SIGGRAPH'75[18] and "Computer Art for Computer People: A Syllabus" in SIGGRAPH'77.[19] Since 1981, SIGGRAPH has sponsored computer art shows during the conference. The support of computer art and research continues to today's SIGGRAPH,

embracing advancements in technology and theory. SIGGRAPH's art gallery has displayed computer art as well as digital and new media art.

By the 1970s, computer art publications and events were prominent throughout the United States. Books such as *Art and the Future*[20] and *Artist and Computer*[21] are important sources to study the history of computer art. *Art and the Future* is a comprehensive guide to the time-based media and technology-influenced art manifestations of that time. It features a variety of movements that include video art, performance art, process art, and a section on computer art. *Artist and Computer* includes texts by computer artists who were active during the 1970s. This publication features a list of thirty-five computer artists, with a majority of them living in the United States. Some of these artists had immigrated to the United States, including Italians Edward Zajec and Giorgini. *Artist and Computer* is a significant record of an international computer art scene in the 1970s.

Uncharted Territory

Computer artists before the personal computers were limited to the challenges of earlier graphics technologies. There was no literature or user manual that could help one make art with a computer. Artists were only able to produce plotted lines, and they dealt with the lack of available standard methods, programs, or languages to make graphics. For many, it was a privilege to be able to use a mainframe computer at all. At this early stage, some artists were able to collaborate directly with scientists. Others had limited access to computers, requiring them to engage specialists run their programs. By the end of the 1960s, many artists and scientists had gained interest in computer art and spontaneously decided to network with peers to further the development of this emerging field. Papers and publications were important means of distribution of these new ideas, because these documents allowed the pioneers to become familiar with the names of each other. It was through a series of these symposia that computer artists met in person and discussed the importance of exploring this new form of art. In recent interview, Colette Bangert[22] recalled the early days of computer art, focusing on the importance of symposia held in different universities across the country.

There was an interest in sharing knowledge and spreading the word of computer art across the United States. According to Bangert, they were not many and "you were lucky if there was another computer artist within your range of miles."[23] For many, including Bangert, it was exciting to be part of a community of artists that networked through computer art symposia. It was natural that these artists wanted to gather together, because they had to create a space for sharing and showcasing their discoveries.

Computer artists came from vastly different backgrounds and oftentimes played many different professional roles. They were researchers of new technologies like at Bell Laboratories; others were college professors in various departments, ranging from sciences to the fine arts. For example, Jeff Bangert is a mathematician at Kansas State; Charles Csuri is in art education at OSU; Robert Mallary (1917–1997) was at the art department at the University of Massachusetts; Aldo Giorgini was in civil engineering at Purdue University. All the aforementioned artists knew one other through symposia and exhibits in which they presented the result of their visual experiments. This network heavily influenced the wide-spreading computer art movement and greatly contributed to what it is today. The computer art movement was unique in that it was mostly based on the resources available in academic or research institutions. The memory of this vibrant art scene is intertwined with the story of Aldo Giorgini.

Notes

1. Nicholas Lambert, "A Critical Examination of 'Computer Art'" (master's thesis, Oxford University, 2007), http://test.lambertsblog.co.uk/wp-content/uploads/2008/02/some-questions-about-computer-art-from-nick-lamberts-thesis.pdf.
2. Annabel Jankel and Rocky Morton, *Creative Computer Graphics* (New York: Cambridge University Press, 1984).
3. Ibid., 26.
4. *Ron Baecker and Lynn Smith, GENESYS: An Interactive Computer-Mediated Animation System,* 16 mm film, 1970, MIT Lincoln Laboratory, http://www.youtube.com/watch?v=GYIPKLxoTcQ.
5. Michael Noll, "The Beginnings of Computer Art in the United States: A Memoir," *Leonardo: Journal of the International Society for the Arts, Sciences and Technology* 27, no. 1 (1994): 39–44.
6. Margit Rosen, ed., *A Little-Known Story About a Movement, a Magazine, and the Computer's Arrival in Art: New Tendencies and Bit International, 1961–1973* (Cambridge, MA: MIT Press), 103.
7. Ibid., 92.
8. Douglas Davis, "The Computer: Final Fusion," in *Art and the Future: A History/Prophecy of the Collaboration Between Science, Technology, and Art* (New York: Praeger Publishers, 1973), 96–105.
9. Jean Dominici DeMaria, "A Study of the Work of Charles Csuri, Computer Artist and Computer Art Educator," (PhD diss., New York University, 1991), 19.
10. Ibid.
11. Joanna Berzowska, "Guest Editorial," *Leonardo: Journal of the International Society for the Arts, Sciences and Technology* 44, no. 4 (2011).
12. DeMaria, "A Study of the Work of Charles Csuri, Computer Artist and Computer Art Educator," 20.
13. Noll, "The Beginnings of Computer Art in the United States: A Memoir," 41.
14. Colette Bangert, interview by author, September 4, 2011.
15. Ibid.
16. Rosen, *A Little-Known Story About a Movement, a Magazine, and the Computer's Arrival in Art.*
17. "Computer Graphics #3," *A Quarterly Report of SIGGRAPH-ACM* 3, no. 3. (1969).

18. Charles Csuri, "Computer Animation." *SIGGRAPH'75 Proceedings of the 2nd annual Conference on Computer Graphics and Interactive Techniques* 9, no. 1 (1975): 92–101, http://dx.doi.org/10.1145/563732.563746.

19. Grace Hertlein, "Computer Art for Computer People: A Syllabus" *SIGGRAPH'77 Proceedings of the 4th annual Conference on Computer Graphics and Interactive Techniques* 9, no. 1 (1977): 249–54, http://dx.doi.org/10.1145/563858.563902.

20. Douglas Davis, "The Computer: Final Fusion."

21. Ruth Leavitt, ed., *Artist and Computer* (New York: Creative Computing Press, 1976).

22. Colette Bangert, interview by author, September 4, 2011.

23. Ibid.

III. FUTURE OF THE COLLECTION

The material legacy that originally remained at the Giorgini residence in Lafayette, Indiana, held an untold life story. Giorgini's studio was kept nearly untouched for twenty years. His complete computer art oeuvre was contained in this one location: documents, artifacts, manuscripts, letters, publications, clippings, printed code, cassette tapes, magnetic tape, CalComp prints, and several screen-printed artworks. Most of the remaining materials at the studio were on paper or Mylar medium, partly because it was the nature of the technology that was available, but also because Giorgini was skeptical of digital media and formats. Thanks to his deliberate decision of making paper copies of every step he completed on the computer in addition to the creation of his own software documentation explaining how his algorithms worked, it was possible to tell a story.

However, by the time I began this research, many materials already showed signs of deterioration and damage from humidity. Before this project, Giorgini's personal papers and art were at risk of disappearing, and with them the story of a pioneer in computer art. After this research was completed, the Giorgini family donated these materials to the Purdue University Virginia Kelly Karnes Archives and Special Collections, where they will be preserved in perpetuity.

Finding Art

With a qualitative framework in mind, I pursued an interpretive approach to the research. I started a blog, where I documented my findings every time I visited the Giorgini residence. Additionally, I kept field notes while I was unveiling the materials. I compiled a purposeful sample of computer art-related documents Every receipt or computer graphic was a new clue for understanding more about Giorgini and his contributions to the world. Gradually, the picture of Aldo Giorgini, someone I had never met, became clearer to me.

My data collection resembled an archeologist finding hidden computer art relics from the 1970s. My first visits focused around a studio table where Giorgini painted most of his CalComp computer plots. Surrounding this table were cabinets and files that contained his civil engineering research manuscripts, printed computer code, punch cards, and several letter-sized CalComp prints. I thoroughly examined every box and cabinet at Giorgini's studio. This task of sorting alone took about seven months. The documents selected were sorted into the following set of categories: computer art-related, correspondence, texts about Giorgini, texts by Giorgini, software manuscripts, teaching materials, professional résumés, and photographs.

Initially, I misjudged the extent of the materials. During my fifth month of exploration, I discovered a blocked room containing an additional sixty boxes. Rolled up inside the boxes were approximately seven hundred paintings and prints on Mylar and paper from the "Stretched Surfaces" period.

Known and unknown art pieces filled the space as I unveiled them. I created a digital catalog of my samples in order to grasp Giorgini's prolific work. The pieces were difficult to handle, given their large dimensions. The amount of 40-by-40-inch to 40-by-120-inch paintings found could only be fully evaluated while standing from a distance. With the help of an assistant, we moved the works and cleaned them. Each of the pieces had debris and mold that had accumulated over the last forty years. We used a dry rag to remove the moldy, crumbled paper that was stuck to the Mylar paintings. Figure 48 shows one of these rolls with the paper damage and displays an example of the process for *Checkerboard*. Some works were destroyed due to water damage; today they only exist as photographs or slides (see Figure 49)

Most of these paintings were rolled up, so I created a special magnet-and-clay wall mount in order to lay them flat and be able to photograph them with a high-resolution digital camera. The artworks were entered into an Excel spreadsheet with embedded images and corresponding metadata so that I could discern if there was redundancy in the sampling

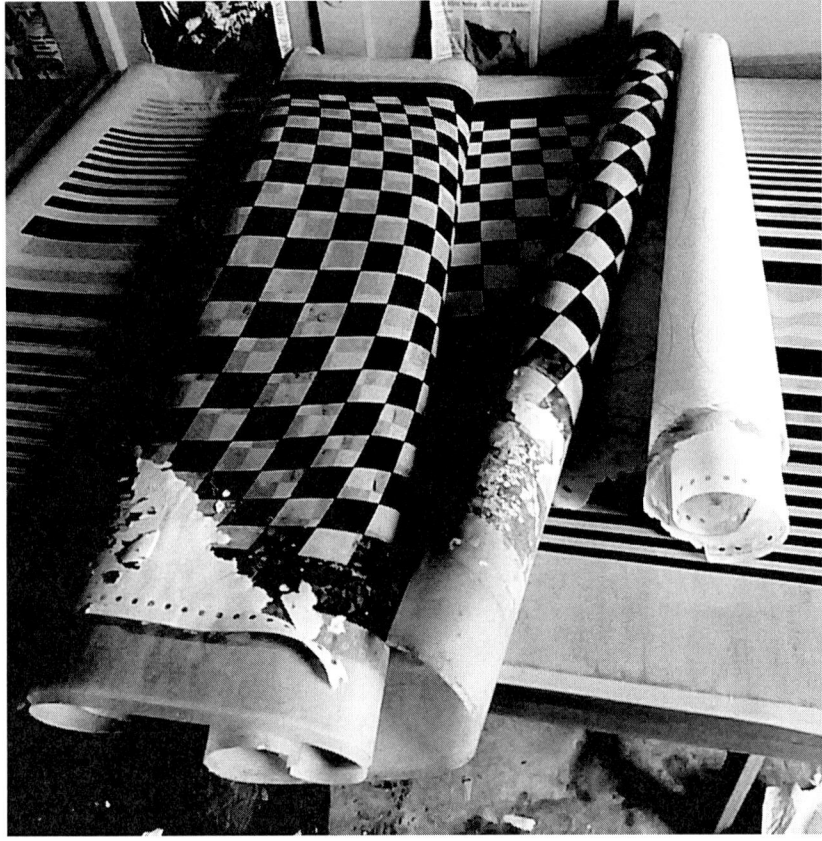

Figure 48. Discovering *Checkerboard* in 2012.

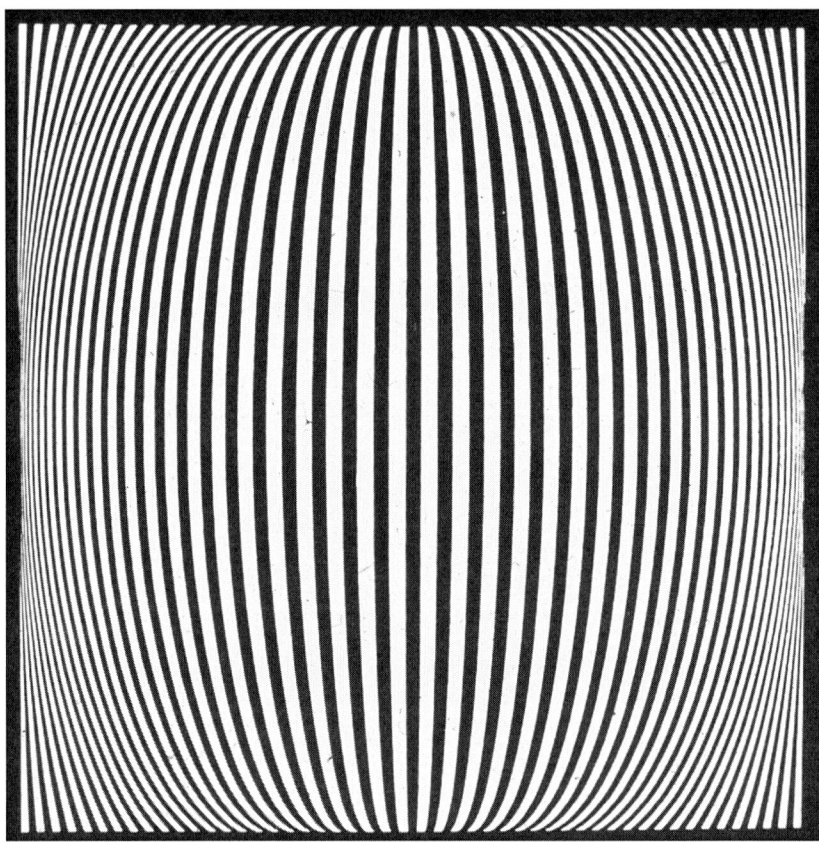

Figure 49. A rendering from the "Ravioli" equation from 1975 that only survived as a 35 mm slide.

process. I established the following criteria in my spreadsheet to sort the work: number, picture, title, year, width, height, media, condition, original/copy, series number, and comments. Although it was not my intent to create a complete catalog of Giorgini's work, it was the only way in which I could study his entire art production. The spreadsheet with embedded images was very useful for study and later for cataloguing at the Purdue University Virginia Kelly Karnes Archives and Special Collections.

I collected four boxes of materials from Giorgini's studio relating specifically to computer art. They included exhibition catalogs, résumés and vitae, letters, art statements, audio recordings, newspaper clippings, and photographs. These materials were instrumental in identifying the dates of the artwork as well as understanding the significance of Giorgini's work in a social context.

Recommendations for Preservation and Display

Through this historic research, this study provides a framework for the future preservation and display of Aldo Giorgini's computer art. Additionally, this study produced a catalog detailing Giorgini's artistic output from 1973 until 1983. The catalog with embedded images and descriptions will aid archivists, curators, and researchers.

This research aimed to be the initial step for the preservation of Giorgini's work, allowing future generations to revisit his contribution. The aim of this study was to explain Giorgini's art in a historical context and to inform future preservation and display practices.

Computer Art Preservation and Display

The archiving of existing materials of early computer art concerns materials that are supported on paper or celluloid (Mylar, magnetic tape, video, or film). In this scenario, the most important conditions for the conservation of these documents is relative to proper archival housing. An archival repository can provide a secure environment for these valued materials to be stored, ensuring in that viewers can have access to it through digital collections, public exhibits, and research rooms.[1] According to Mary Lynn Ritzenthaler, temperature and relative humidity are some of the most important factors in the storage environments, and can speed up or slow down the process of deterioration of the material. High humidity can, for example, accelerate the "deteriorative chemical reactions and encourage mold growth."[2] Low humidity would result in the drying of the materials and cause a paper to become fragile or affect the photographic emulsions from pictures. Moderately cool environments are preferred for storage. Keeping the temperature between 35° F and 65° F can ensure a long life for the materials. These environmental conditions are optimal for pieces that are encased in cellulose.[3]

All of Giorgini's works are supported on paper or Mylar, and thus it is recommended that Giorgini's materials are stored in a moderately cool environment. The Mylar and paper paintings preferably should be stored in a flat file, but they may be rolled up. Some of Giorgini's paintings are 112 inches wide, and it might be difficult to find space or a flat file of such dimensions. The majority of the works found at the studio were rolled up, which in some instances caused serious damage. Giorgini secured the Mylar and paper rolls closed with masking tape. Some works have traces of adhesive from deteriorated tape, causing the work to glue to itself. Although some of the artworks came in contact with water in the early 2000s and subsequently were damaged, many survived. Giorgini's use of Mylar as the media for his paintings was a fortunate decision for history, as many paper copies were destroyed under these circumstances.

One possible approach to display Giorgini's work is as he originally installed it, using photographic references to reconstruct them. Photocopying the artwork could allow one to reconstruct pieces such as *Sculptural Forms* or *Fiat Lux*. The *Surfaces* series could also be reinstalled in modules as displayed in *CE-X-hibit* (Figure 18). The original paintings also can be displayed on a wall using magnets. The works made with the Tektronix from 1982 can be reprinted as well. The slides found were scanned at a high resolution and can be restored to their original size. Curators may use the catalog of works and decide upon a list of works to be displayed. Giorgini's work was predominantly visual and perceptual, and it would be at the discretion of each curator to select the works that he or she considers relevant. This study presented theoretical frameworks in which to aid in the understanding of Giorgini's themes. Supporting documents, such as manuscripts or computer codes, also could be exhibited in display cases so patrons may better understand the context of the work. Based on these elements of display, I curated a retrospective of Giorgini's work at the Patti and Rusty Rueff Galleries in Yue-Kong Pao Hall in 2013 (Figure 50). The original artworks were shown chronologically and complemented with digital slideshows and documentation.

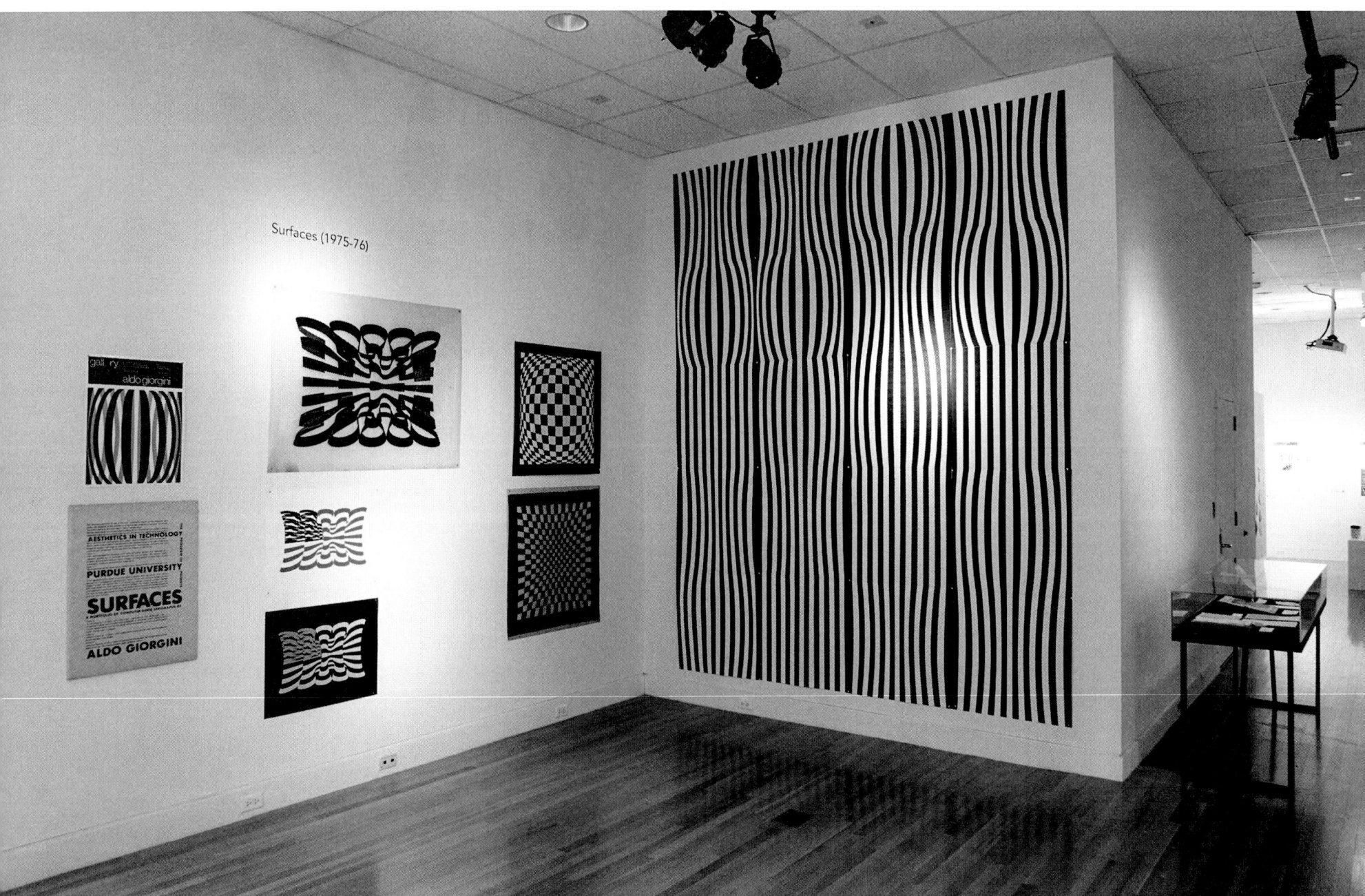

Future work could include the re-creation of Giorgini's computer art frameworks using modern technologies to allow viewers or users to understand his software by experimenting with it. These re-creations could explore the use of emerging interactive technologies or interfaces to make Giorgini's contribution more approachable to newer generations of enthusiasts.

The outcomes of this study were a biography and a catalog of complete computer artworks by Aldo Giorgini.[4] Most of these artworks remained unknown for almost forty years and were unveiled by this research. This project played an important role in the preservation of Giorgini's materials, through their inclusion in the Purdue University Virginia Kelly Karnes Archives and Special Collections. The materials include computer art themes, such as documents concerned with the production and execution of the software art, physical outputs, prints, and related materials. These findings will be preserved and made accessible for future researchers of media art history. Collections such as the Giorgini papers will provide challenges as well as opportunities for archivists, artists, or curators who seek to make these materials accessible for generations to come.

Notes

1. Mary Ritzenthaler, "Creating a Preservation Environment," in *Preserving Archives and Manuscripts* (Chicago: The Society of American Archivists, 2010), 109–51.
2. Ibid., 115.
3. Ibid., 120.
4. Unfortunately, this book can only include a limited selection of images, but all will be accessible through the Purdue University Virginia Kelly Karnes Archives and Special Collections.

Figure 50. Retrospective exhibit of Aldo Giorgini in 2013. Curated by the author.

IV. SELECTED TEXTS BY ALDO GIORGINI

FIELDS (1975)

Soon after the advent of the digital computer, its users have occasionally played with its output facilities to obtain print-outs or drawings which we could call "visual experiments."

The "mediate" nature of the computer facilities constitutes an intriguing challenge to everybody inclined both to programming and to the visual arts.

The word *Computer Art* was soon born, with semi-magical overtones for the uninitiated and with some confusion or bias for the user himself.

If we limit our attention to digital computers, a first classification of the *computer visual arts* would most naturally be made according to the type of output device. In fact Cathode Ray Tubes (CRT), printers, plotters . . . , have distinct differences as media for art work. What is easily achieved with one, may be either impossible, or time-wasting or awkward to achieve with the others. Each output device has its own graphical characteristics which, once fully understood and fully exploited, may yield an incredible amount of possible forms.

In the present report the output facility under consideration is the CALCOMP plotter. The drawing instrument is the ink pen, and the graphical element is a line, be it ostensibly curved or polygonal.

Once the graphical output device is specified, one may further distinguish between autonomous and synergetic computer art.

Autonomous computer art is here defined as applying when the output of the machine is considered the final form of the art piece. In the case where the output needs further intervention by the artist in order to produce the final art piece, the term of *synergetic computer art* (or computer aided art) will apply.

The two definitions seem to me necessary in order to accommodate two equally valid attitudes toward the computer use in art: the attitude of the "purist", who will program the machine to do everything and who will feel fulfilled only if the machine output does not need further "contamination" by human hands, and the more relaxed attitude of complementing the "abilities" of the artist.

Notice that these attitudes should not be confused with, albeit they may be correlated to, the degree of mastery of the tools of the "medium" by the artist. If a given art piece may be produced either autonomously or synergetically, the "purist" will meet the challenge by sometime virtuosistic feats of programming, while the "non-purist" will reduce the programming complexities and plan for personal intervention on the machine output.

My personal attitude is toward the synergetic approach to computer art, without excluding the autonomous. In fact one may, somehow facetiously, define a "degree of synergism" and consider the autonomous approach as a synergetic approach with zero degree of synergism. . . . In other words, the strictly autonomous approach seems to me too intransigent and too limited to be continuously held. In fact, besides conditioning the inspiration to what the machine can do, no matter how forcibly, it may lead to incredibly intricate programs and extravagant computer time (both CP and PP) requirements.

As far as the Calcomp output device is concerned, with the limitation of black on white drawings with round penpoints of different sizes, the real "abilities" of the machine consist in the production of lines of uniform thickness with unrestricted curvature variations. Drawings that the machine takes fifteen minutes to draw, would take literally hundreds of hours by an expert hand, with comparable results.

On the other hand colored areas defined by somehow complex contours may take incredible programming times (justifiable only for multipurpose programs) and still require several hours of drawing by the output device.

As an application of the program presented in this report, computer and hand will be used synergetically at various degrees.

A further classification of computer art can be formulated in order to dispel prejudices about the amount of chance that may be present in computer drawings. Accordingly, I will define *intentional computer art* and *serendipitous computer art*. "Canned" programs are available in which, by simply specifying the numerical value of a certain number of parameters, one can often obtain a pleasant drawing. In this case it is very difficult to estimate the degree of intentionality of the user. If the user knows very well the "mechanism" of the program and what all those parameters mean, it may be assumed that the result was intentional. But a user who plays with the program by changing the value of the parameters at random, may hardly be considered as intentionally producing the drawing. These serendipitous results may be considered at the same level of the results due to programming errors or machine misfunctioning. They may suggest new avenues of exploration and constitute, therefore, invaluable raw material for further study, but they can hardly be called "art," unless we decide to call art any *a posteriori* choice.

Practice with a particular program may lead the user to very sophisticated and mediate results which may baffle the uninitiated viewer. Some examples of computer optical art, in which perceptional effects are used to create new visual experiences are presented in the applications.

The last classification of computer art can be based on whether the approach is deterministic or statistical. Accordingly in *deterministic computer art* the artist will use the computer by specifying all the movements that the pen must perform on the paper, while *stochastic computer art* will refer to those computer works in whose programs the random number generator is used.

I point at the possible confusion, into which the reader may incurr [*sic*], between the adjective seredipitous [*sic*] and stochastic. They are not synonimous [*sic*] because statistical methods may be used intentionally, with full knowledge of the statistical order of the result. In my opinion the indiscriminate use of the random number generator may create confusion and cast a shade of a doubt on the intentionality of the result, on the other side its skillful use may add a new dimension to computographical art.

I will touch, at last, a subject that has presented some problem in the past. A computer drawing may have been made by a person with a program formulated by another person and programmed by another person again. Who is the artist? In a program like the one presented in this report several intermediate steps lay between the idea and the final product. Step I: a very broad idea is formulated mathematically. Step II: a computer program is written. Step III: the program is then used to implement a particular idea. Step IV: the computer drawing that results is sometimes completed by the ideator of the drawing (or by aides). It seems to me obvious that the artist is the ideator of the drawing (the "particular idea" of Step III) but it must be realized that the program that has been used has had a strong influence on how the artist operates. The program is more than a medium: it is a "programme" with build-in directions which, no matter how open, still compel the artist to move with some constraints or on along some perspective, that are part of the original idea of the program.

I, therefore, suggest a list of credits as presented in the following example which refer to figure 21.

Negative Reflection
by Aldo Giorgini
Computer-aided Drawing
Drawn with the use of a CALCOMP PLOTTER
with the program "Fields"
(ideated and mathematically formulated by Aldo Giorgini)
Programmed in FORTRAN language by W. C. Chen

The Idea:

EQUIPOTENTIAL LINES OF A PHYSICAL FIELD WITHIN SPECIFIED BOUNDARIES

Families of lines have a strong appeal to the imagination of anybody with inclination to geometrization.

The gradual variation of curvature along each line, and the gradual differentiation of each line from the other lines, constitute an infinite source of aesthetical possibilities for exploitation.

Equipotential lines of physical fields, yield themselves to innumerable configurations, which have the property of being clearly envisioned by anybody with some rudiments of physics and which could easily be computer simulated by whomever possesses the mathematical tools for formulating the idea into mathematical terms and the knowledge for programming the mathematical model.

The computer program here presented wants to simulate a physical field by means of its equipotential lines, once some equipotential boundaries are given and a distribution of field sources is imagined as being distributed over part of (or all) the domain of interest.

The potential difference between any two successive equipotential lines either may be kept constant or gradually varying according to some continuous law, so as to generate a feeling of continuity in the "density" of the lines in the field, or may be varied briskly for special purposes.

If the above program were carried out at the letter, a considerable amount of computer time would be required by all but the simplest configurations. In fact, such endeavors would require the solution of partial differential equations in two-dimensional domains at an incredible amount of geometrical points in order to guarantee a desired smoothness in the flow of the curves. The short cut that is presented here will generate a fictitious potential surface $Z=Z(x,y)$ (whose intersections with the plane Z-const are the equipotential lines) by means of elementary potential surfaces which qualitatively simulate the geometry of physical fields. The end product of the operations performed on the elementary potential surfaces will closely resemble the geometrical representation of the physical field.

The rationale is based on the fact that for purely visual purposes any family of curves that fills a field and continuously modifies itself as to embrace the boundaries, will be perceived as a field no matter how far from the true physical field is the form of visual experiment. On the other side it is always possible to find a suitable distribution of field sources that makes the visual experiment coincide with a true physical field.

The plan of the present study is the following. Some zero-potential field generating "boundary-source elements" are defined. By means of these, it will be possible to create a virtually limitless amount of boundary configurations with two possible values of the boundary potential: zero and one.

EXPERIMENTS IN COMPUTER VISUALIZATION (1975)

A report on the homonymous project | *Sponsored by the Aesthetics in Technology Program of Purdue University*

Submitted by Aldo Giorgini

THE OBJECTIVES OF THE PROJECT WERE

first: to conduct visual experiments on surfaces, by means of computer graphics techniques

second: to conduct fluid mechanics experiments by means of computer graphic techniques

third: to organize a series of lectures by well-known computer artists

VISUAL EXPERIMENTS ON SURFACES

The set of experiments that have been run was based on the following recipe:

a: take a suitable surface amenable to mathematical formulation;

b: draw "simple" signs on the surfaces;

c: project the signs on a plane.

The rationale underlying the above recipe was the following: since monocular vision is a two-dimensional projection of three-dimensional surfaces, a three-dimensional effect of a two-dimensional drawing can be achieved by compelling the viewer to "organize" the two-dimensional material presented to him. The hint given to the viewer is that the two-dimensional signs that he sees are in reality plane projections of "simple" signs on a curved surface.

The easily recognizable signs that have been used are:
- stripes
- checkerboard patterns
- circles
- the American flag

The surfaces that have been used are:
- The "ravioli" surface $z = xy(1-x)(1-y)$ within the region $(0 < x < 1, 0 < y < 1)$
- a complex flag-like surface
- other surfaces (in the process of being studied)

A very interesting outcome of the first experiments, that has lifted the importance of the research, has come about when I tried to superimpose two different (semi-transparent) surfaces. The three-dimensional effect of the result was strongly enhanced when the two surfaces were superimposed in their natural perspective order. But when the order was inverted (what I call anti-perspective), interesting perceptive phenomena occurred. Apparently our brain reorganizes the material in such a way as to make sense of these stimuli, and the objects are interpreted in very surprising ways.

The results of these experiments are going to be published in the near future as
- a silkscreen portfolio of 8 prints (limited edition of 100 prints);
- a research report.

The silkscreen portfolio is under production at present.

COMPUTOGRAPHICAL EXPERIMENTS IN "DESCRIPTIVE HYDROMECHANICS"

The considerations that prompted this research have been

- the desperately little knowledge that still is available about rotational motion of viscous fluids;

- the incommensurably meager help that advanced mathematical tools give to the understanding of fluid motion;

- the hope that nevertheless fluid motion may be explained by simple mechanisms (hidden by the complexity of their mathematical formulation and by the very mediate ways we visualize fluid flows).

The problem that has been considered as representative of this descriptive approach has been the two-dimensional flow of a viscous fluid past a non-rotating circular cylinder.

It is well known that as the Reynolds number increases from zero to a value below the inception of the "turbulent" wake, four different fluid configurations are observable

conf 1 – the fluid flows around the cylinder without separating from it;

conf 2 – separation occurs with the formation of standing vortices behind the cylinder;

conf 3 – the wake oscillates slightly;

conf 4 – the vortices behind the cylinder are shed (Karman wake).

By means of experimental data available in published literature, and with an eye to the physical constraints of the phenomenon, I have "fitted" a stream function according to a simplified model. According to this model to the ostensible differences between conf 1 and conf 2 and the ostensible differences between conf 3 and 4 are not brought about by differences in hydromechanical behavior. If we call

mech 1 = conf 1 or conf 2

mech 2 = conf 3 or conf 4

mech 2 is a perturbed oscillatory form of mech 1.

The insight is the mechanisms has been hidden by the fact that streaklines (the most common source of our visual experience of fluid flows) have intricate appearance and may suggest more complex mechanisms than necessary for an understanding of fluid flows.

A detailed presentation of these findings will be available in the form of a separate report in the near future.

[This is the second part of a commentary on the Computer Art Day, held at Purdue on April 24. The first part, "Harold Cohen 'Tools'", appeared in STPP number twenty eight, June 1975. The excerpt from Cohen's lecture will be referred to as (I) in the following note.]

Computer Art is far from being a popular word among most artists and art critics. The reasons for this state of affairs are many, some justifiable, some not.

FIRST: the term Computer Art does not refer to a current, to a style, or to any manifesto-like statement of intentions made by a group of artists, according to aesthetic, political, social, and cultural criteria. The term refers to all those art forms that use the computer in any of the stages that lead to the final product. The term *Art by Computer* may be a more acceptable form to some, albeit terminology is hardly the battlefield for most informed detractors of Computer Art. Nevertheless the term lends itself to some speculations that may clarify some objections to the subject matter to which the term applies. Consider, as an example, the alternate art form that could be called *Art by Hand* (and for this particular example let us assume for the moment that the Computer Art product has not been "contaminated" by human hand). The strictest application of the definition would exclude most art forms but finger-painting and claymolding. As soon as the hand is allowed to handle a tool for the production of an artpiece, the stretching of the definition of Art by Hand may easily be seen to have an upper limit in the uncontaminated Computer Art.

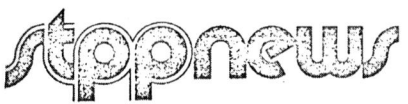

An Interdisciplinary Newsletter on Science, Technology, Public Policy and Society

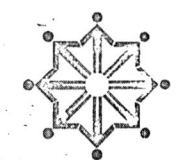

NUMBER TWENTYNINE — PURDUE UNIVERSITY — SEPTEMBER 1975

IS TECHNOLOGY ASSESSMENT A SOCIAL SCIENCE?
MICHAEL COHEN

Emphatically yes, according to panelists in a symposium on technology assessment at the Philosophy of Science Association biennial conference held at Notre Dame University in early November. The panelists—Profs. Henry Skolimowski of the University of Michigan, Tom Settle of the University of Guelph, and Joseph Agassi of Boston University—debated the social, ethical, and political implications of technology assessment in terms that are worth special note because they mark an important change in the philosophical attitude toward the scientific status of technology assessment.

Bluntly put, the panelists said that, contrary to the views of many scientists and engineers, technology assessment is not a matter of seeing whether the technology works but rather of seeing what the impact on society is when the technology is put to use. The key skills required are therefore not those of the physical and biological sciences but those of the social sciences.

Skolimowski set the stage by claiming that there is no possibility of valid technology assessment unless it is constructed out of the philosophy of technology. He defined the philosophy of technology as a systematic examination of the underlying assumptions of technological civilization. According to this view, technological experts are the least able to conduct technological assessments since they uncritically accept all the assumptions on which technology is based.

(Continued on Page 10)

BLACK BOXES AND ART
PART II: OF CHISELS AND COMPUTERS

by Aldo Giorgini
School of Civil Engineering
Purdue University

[This is the second part of a commentary on the Computer Art Day, held at Purdue on April 24. The first part, "Harold Cohen 'Tools'", appeared in STPP number twenty-eight, June 1975. The excerpt from Cohen's lecture will be referred to as (I) in the following note.]

Computer Art is far from being a popular word among most artists and art critics. The reasons for this state of affairs are many, some justifiable, some not.

FIRST: the term Computer Art does not refer to a current, to a style, or to any manifesto-like statement of intentions made by a group of artists, according to aesthetic, political, . . . criteria. The term refers to all those art forms that use the computer in any of the stages that lead to the final product. The term Art by Computer may be a more acceptable form to some, albeit terminology is hardly the battlefield for most informed detractors of Computer Art. Nevertheless the term lends itself to some speculations that may clarify some objections to the subject matter to which the term applies. Consider, as an example, the alternate art form that could be called Art by Hand (and for this particular example let us assume for the moment that the Computer Art product has not been "contaminated" by human hand). The strictest application of the definition would exclude most art forms but fingerpainting and claymolding. As soon as the hand is allowed to handle a tool for the production of an artpiece, the stretching of

(cont. on page 12)

Figure 51. Cover of the newsletter in which this text was originally published in 1975.

SECOND: In order to clarify some of the steps in the production of Computer Art for the uninitiated let us review briefly the role of the computer in it. According to a very appealing definition given by Cohen (I) the computer is a "virtual machine", in the sense that its role is similar to a construction set. The real machine is the program, which instructs the computer on how to assemble itself in order to perform some operations, among which the driving of output machines are included. The output machines, in turn, may be able to perform any kind of drawing, brushing, photosensitizing, lathing, sound transmitting . . . operations. The program is therefore the link between man and computer, via the instructions contained in it (usually in the FORTRAN language). The most remarkable feature of the computer is without doubt its ability of rapidly performing over and over the same series of operations under the instruction of the so-called DO statement. The same instructions are repeated by the computer until the data given by the programmer are exhausted. But what the machine does is exactly what the programmer instructs it to do. When one says that the programmer may instruct the computer to make . . . "its own decisions", one says no more than: the programmer has been directing it to draw exactly the 1015th, say, number in a list of numbers that have been randomly chosen and have been stored in sequential order in the memory of the computer. This decision-making of the computer is analogous to the decision-making of a person instructed [programmed] to walk on the streets of a city with the convention of either turning left, or right, or proceeding at the intersections according to whether the haircolor of the first woman he (or she) sees at the intersection is blond, brown, or black. In this case, the computer is in reality used as a guinea pig: since it can perform very fast operations that would take literally years of hand computation, we can repeat the same experiment with different random parameters and then make decisions on the result, still, maybe, with the use of the computer.

Seen in this light the role of the computer is analogous to the role of the hand+tool, and this becomes more evident if we think of the feasible alternative to writing the program in FORTRAN: speaking directly into a microphone which serves as input device for the computer.

To summarize this second point, some of the appealing features of the computer use in art are:

(1) the virtual elimination of the artist's hand;
(2) the rapidity of its performance;
(3) the generality of the program machine;
(4) the statistical (decision-like) capabilities;
(5) the possibility of reproducing uncountable copies of the same output

Contrary to other tools (and, perhaps, just because the computer becomes a hand+tool) it has become traditional of Computer Art to have to justify itself by answering to the question "Could this be done by any other tool?" [Notice that nobody would object to the use of the compass for drawing a circle, or to the use of the ruler to draw a straight line]; and, again, to justify the above features against the question, "Couldn't this be done by hand?" (and here hand means hand + any-other-tool-but-the-computer). The answer is, obviously, that everything can be done by hand. But this is not the real problem. The problem is the *realistic* feasibility of doing by hand the same things that the computer can do rather easily. It is surprising that the same people that do not object in spending hundreds of thousands of dollars for an architectural sculpture that has never seen the hand of its "maker", should object to the fact that between the idea and the final product there has been the intervention of the computer. Still the feature extension → elimination of the artist's hand is perhaps the most easily accepted print by the Computer Art detractors. The most important issue, the extension → elimination of the artist's creativity, will be touched upon later.

At this point it may be interesting, in order to fall back onto the Computer Art Day, to touch upon some pitfalls into which computer artists often slide and which may constitute grounds for the suspicion by the art world.

The generality of the program-machine with its very versatile subroutines constitutes an almost irresistible temptation toward the creation of a "universal" program, able to do everything and of possible use to everybody. This route is the more tempting if one thinks that, ironically, the preparation of a somehow complex program (as general purpose programs are) requires a very long time to prepare and to debug. The temptation here is evident: how can I (after having spent so much time in preparing the program) use it as many times as desired with ostensibly different outputs? These programs, no matter how general, are still very strongly conditioned by the constraints of their inventor and are very little helpful to other people with ideas of their own (they may still have some didactic value). An analogous situation would be the one of trying to use a grain grinding machine for the purpose of flying. While this aspect of programming leads, on one hand, some people to get more deeply involved with the technical aspects of the subroutines used for art, and eventually creating elaborate program-machines for doing this and that (and the Computer Art Day showed that some people are chiefly interested in these technical aspects), on the other hand it encourages other people with little knowledge about programming to use these programs without realizing that, by so doing, they oblige more to the constraints of another person's imagination than to the constraints of the computer.

Another virtual pitfall is constituted by the use of the random number generator. Statistical effects can obviously be planned and controlled, but the indiscriminate use of the random number generator can lead to outputs which are entirely serendipitous and, especially if the program is not one's own, it may reduce the artist's intervention to the mere pseudodemiurgic choice between elected and condemned drawings among the plethora of outputs. This attitude obviously gives ground to the suspicions that lead to the

THIRD POINT: "Isn't the computer used as an extension of the artist's creativity?" It is surprising that the accusation of extension of creativity goes usually pace to pace with the statement that nothing really new has happened in the field of Computer Art. In the July 15 Bulletin of the Computer Arts Society, PAGE 36, Mr. Michael Thompson answers, in an article entitled "Not Flocking to the Computers?", to a statement by Robert Mallary (PAGE 34) about his surprise that Op artists have not flocked to the computer, and how much is still to be said with Op Art. In the answer, Mr. Thompson states that

a. computer work is non-visual and the use of computers appeals only to those people who have a tendency toward geometry, which, according to Mr. Thompson, is really bad for computer artists, but not for the traditional artists, in fact

b. the hand work (by means of templates) of Bridget Riley, (compared against Noll's computer drawings) was done "ten years ago, so why bother? And without a computer – so why use them at all? My only answer is: use computers not so much to produce art but to test and develop ideas on visual topics. Since not all ideas can be applied, but only rather precisely formulated ones, and because it is rather difficult to describe artistic problems in this way, 'computer art' is likely to appeal mainly to people who happen to find computers fascinating, and to those who want to understand the visual in the same exactly defined way that computers operate."

Instead of commenting on point *b* I offer the following paraphrase referring to a fictitious first marble sculpture by chisel with respect to traditional clay molding: "But so-and-so did it one hundred years ago, so why bother? And without a chisel—so why use them at all? . . . Chisel sculpting is likely to appeal mainly to people who happen to find chisels fascinating . . . . "

As far as point *a* is concerned, besides the fact that it is not true that all Computer Art is geometric [see, e.g., Colette S. Bangert and Charles J. Bangert, "Experiences in Making Drawings by Computer and by Hand", *Leonardo*, Vol. 1, No. 4, Autumn 1974], Mr. Thompson decides that all art stems from ". . . the continued visual monitoring of how the job is going, and the immense freedom to change to more-or-less any colour or form at any stage." This is obviously one of the extremes of the actual mental and bodily process of rendering an artwork, the other extreme of this continuum being the process of entirely formulating and rearranging mental pictures on visual phenomena, and to come up with its accurate graphical representation at a later time, after the stage of the mental (and perhaps manual) sketches is completed.

Obviously Computer Art is closer to the second approach, and some of the prerequisites for a successful production are

a. the ability of formulating and rearranging mental pictures on visual phenomena;

b. the ability of formulating mathematically the mental objects;

c. the ability of conversing with the computer.

In other words: it takes talent and effort, just as in the case of the chisel. This may be considered esoteric by some, virtuosistic by others, but both adjectives hide in themselves one concept: unfamiliarity with a process. Anybody who has experienced the process of learning a foreign language knows how miraculous the oral formulation of thoughts looks in the initial stages of communication attempts.

In conclusion it seems to me that the position of antagonism against Computer Art, while justified by the somehow limited production of the few people conversant with the computer as an art tool, is untenable, just as untenable is the position of considering Art by Computer as "different" from any other way of producing art. The word Computer Art will die away and what will be left is Art or non-art whether done by computer or not.

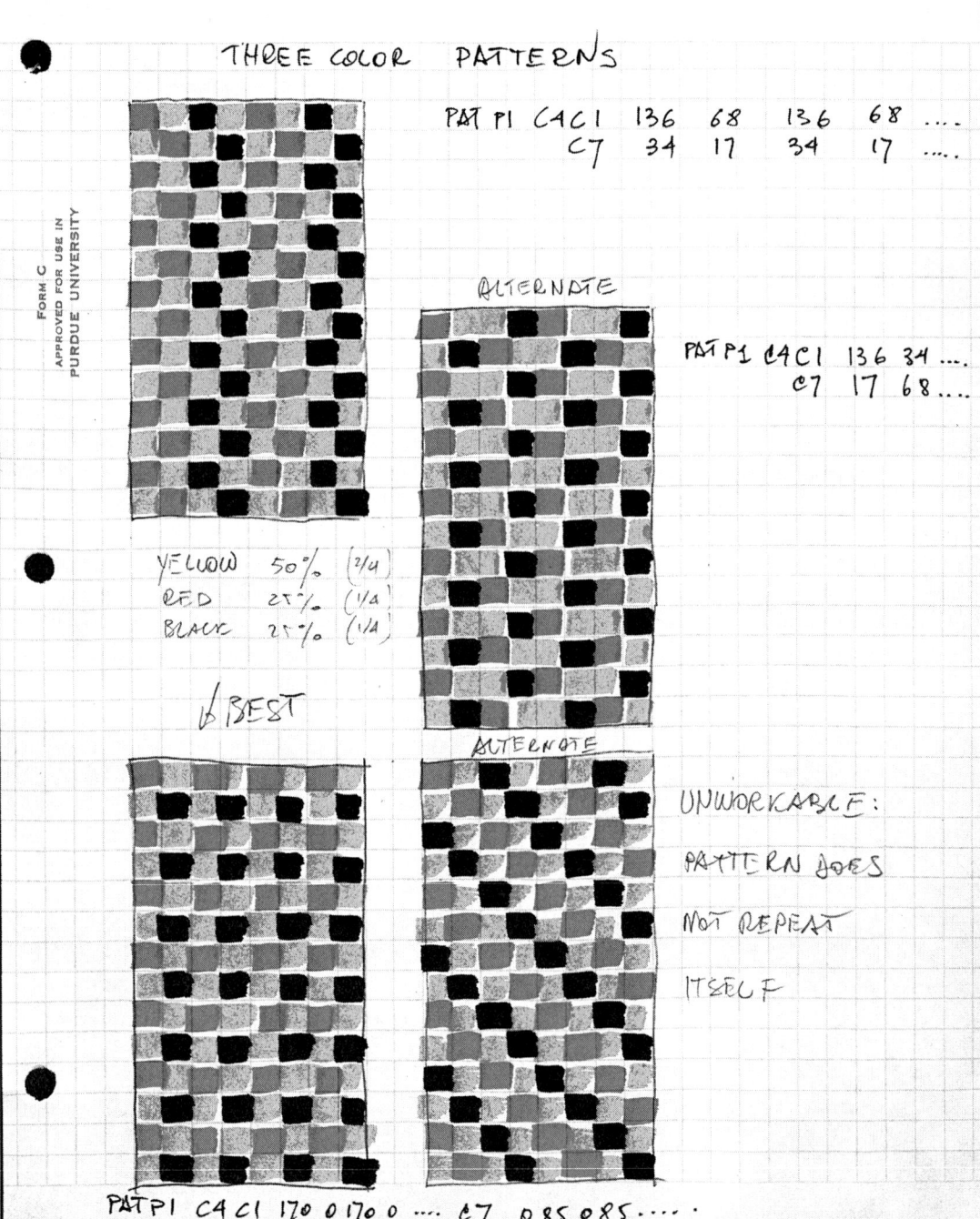

THREE COLOR PATTERNS

PAT PI C4 C1   136   68   136   68 ....
         C7   34   17   34   17 ....

ALTERNATE

PAT P1 C4 C1   136   34 ....
          C7   17   68 ....

YELLOW   50%   (2/4)
RED   25%   (1/4)
BLACK   25%   (1/4)

✓ BEST

ALTERNATE

UNWORKABLE:

PATTERN DOES

NOT REPEAT

ITSELF

PAT PI C4 C1 170 0 170 0 .... C7 0 85 0 85 .....

FORM C
APPROVED FOR USE IN
PURDUE UNIVERSITY

Figure 52. This sketch illustrates Giorgini's intent of creating new colors through mathematical distributed patterns.

PALETTE (1980)

1.1 Presentation

The study presented in this report is only a small portion of a project that has as its aim the determination of the pressure and shear stress distribution on a solid surface, caused by the splash of a drop on a liquid film covering the surface.

Since this goal is almost impossible to achieve either analytically or experimentally, the aim of the project has been set, therefore, in terms of the *numerical* determination of pressure and shear stress. The reliability of the results is nevertheless dependent on the positive comparison of the numerical results with experimental data.

Since most of the experimental data are in photographic form, that is since detailed measurements are not available but several accurate time-release photographs of drop splashes are available, the proposal originating the research here reported had suggested a comparison of the photographs with pictures obtained by suitable manipulation of the computational results. This suggestion is now under implementation, but it is instructive to examine in detail what the above comparison entails in order to put the present study in its right perspective.

In order to illustrate a three-dimensional object in photograph-like fashion, it is first necessary to schematize the object. One such schematization is the approximation of the object to a polyhedron. In the case of an axisymmetric drop slash, the facets of the polyhedral surface are trapezes. This polyhedron is then subjected to one or more light sources, is "observed", that is, it is projected on a plane called the picture plane, from a given observation point.

The picture so obtained is colored with its color attributes (depending on the color of the light sources and of the color of the surface of the object to be illustrated).

Assume that you have at hand a Tektronix 4027 color terminal and a fast computer, with minimal software for the picture, so minimal, in fact, that a color palette is not available and only eight colors, definable at will from a "wider" palette of 64 colors, can be simultaneously used. What should you do in order to solve the problem? Obviously you would start by creating a palette.

This is in fact the object of the study presented in this report. Actually, the report is slightly more general. It tries to create alternate palettes with all possible colors of which a subset of colors (abridged palettes), among which the grey palettes and other special purpose palettes.

Other reports will deal with the other aspects of the project.

1.2 The Raw Material

The pictorial capabilities of the Tektronix 4027 can be summarized as follows:

A. At most, eight "basic" colors, C0, C1, C2, C3, C4, C5, C6, C7, obtainable at will from a virtual1 palette of 64 colors, can be used simultaneously on the screen;

B. Any one of the screen pixels can be addressed at one time by any one of the above colors;

C. The intensity of a color at any given pixel cannot be changed independently of the intensity of the rest of the screen (the terminal has only one intensity regulator for the whole screen).

D. Patterns can be designed by using any number of the basic colors, C0, . . . , C7 in an 8 x 14 matrix.

1.3 The Criterion for Palette Implementation

Given the above data, it is possible to design patterns that will look like colors, once seen some distance from the screen. These patterns should possess the characteristic of looking as uniform as possible and, therefore, as little pattern-like as possible. They will be called color-patterns from now on. This is the only criterion used in what follows.

I. THE COLOR PATTERNS

2.1 Basic Colors and Mixtures

In this section we will assume that the basic colors in the Tektronix 4027 are, as they are usually defined,

C0	White
C1	Red
C2	Green
C3	Blue
C4	Yellow
C5	Cyan
C6	Magenta
C7	Black

If they were not, the following statements would provide the above definitions:

!MAP	C0	0	100	0
!MAP	C1	120	50	100
!MAP	C2	240	50	100
!MAP	C3	0	50	100
!MAP	C4	180	50	100
!MAP	C5	300	50	100
!MAP	C6	60	50	100
!MAP	C7	0	0	0

The Tektronix 4027 color double cone (see Appendix A) is then transformed in a double hexagonal pyramid as shown in Figure 1.

The basic colors have been assigned coherently with the illustration of Appendix A.

The most interesting aspect of the double pyramid is that it could be imagined as the union of six tetrahedra, as shown in Figure 2.[2] The tetrahedra are regular if the distance C0-C7 is equal to a side of the base hexagon.

STRETCH (1981)³

PART ONE

THE STRECHING OF AN ELASTIC MEMBRANE

TO A RIGID FRAME

By Aldo Giorgini

THE IDEA

In the early years of my life, when I was in Eritrea, Africa, I enjoyed stretching pelts on wooden frames. The pelts, usually kids' and occasionally wildcats', were salted for immediate preservation and then sent to a tannery. I recall my interest in stretching the pelts in unorthodox fashions (to the objection of some experts) in order to create interesting regions between the pelt and the frame of the stretcher.

I was not aware at that time (I was nine years old) that I was exercising some aesthetic judgment similar to the one of the arts. It is not surprising that I should "resonate" at the sight of the stretching of the Vitruvius Man performed by Csuri by means of computational techniques.

To be my "feeling" of stretching was somehow disturbed by some features of Csuri's deformation of the Vitruvius Man. First: there seemed to be no rational point for the pinch points (the points that pinch the membrane on which the Vitruvius Man is drawn); second: some regions of the membrane did not seem to behave as an elastic medium.

Notice that these observations only describe my reactions to Csuri's drawings, and, while they are no aesthetical critique for these drawings, they surely constitute the behavioral foundation of my aesthetics of elastic deformations.

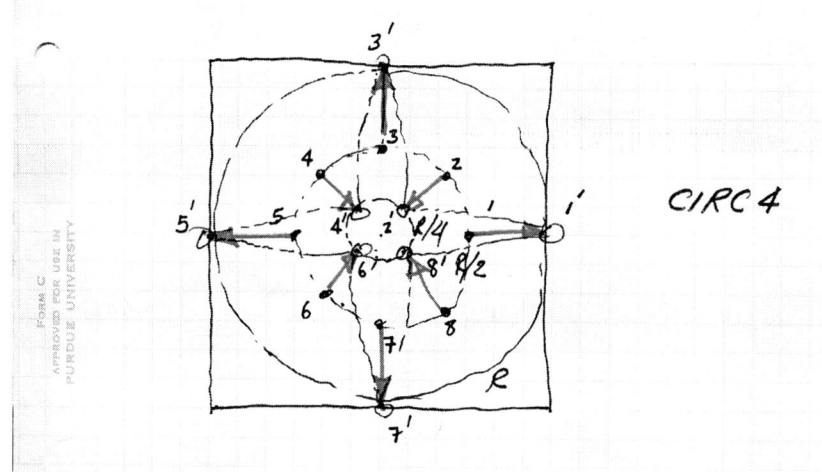

Figure 53. A handmade sketch revealing the principles of the Stretch software.

The opportunity to approach the visual problem of the stretching of an elastic membrane presented itself during a research project in descriptive fluid mechanics and therefore I devoted some time to the formulation and to the development of the idea.

The problem at hand is the following: given a finite elastic membrane on which lines are drawn, pinch the membrane at a given number of points (the BASE POINTS) and stretch it to the (same number of) given points on the stretcher (the FRAME POINTS).

The solution of this problem by the techniques of the theory of elasticity is beyond hope, since the distribution of the stresses in the membrane is strongly influenced by the presence of the boundaries (the size

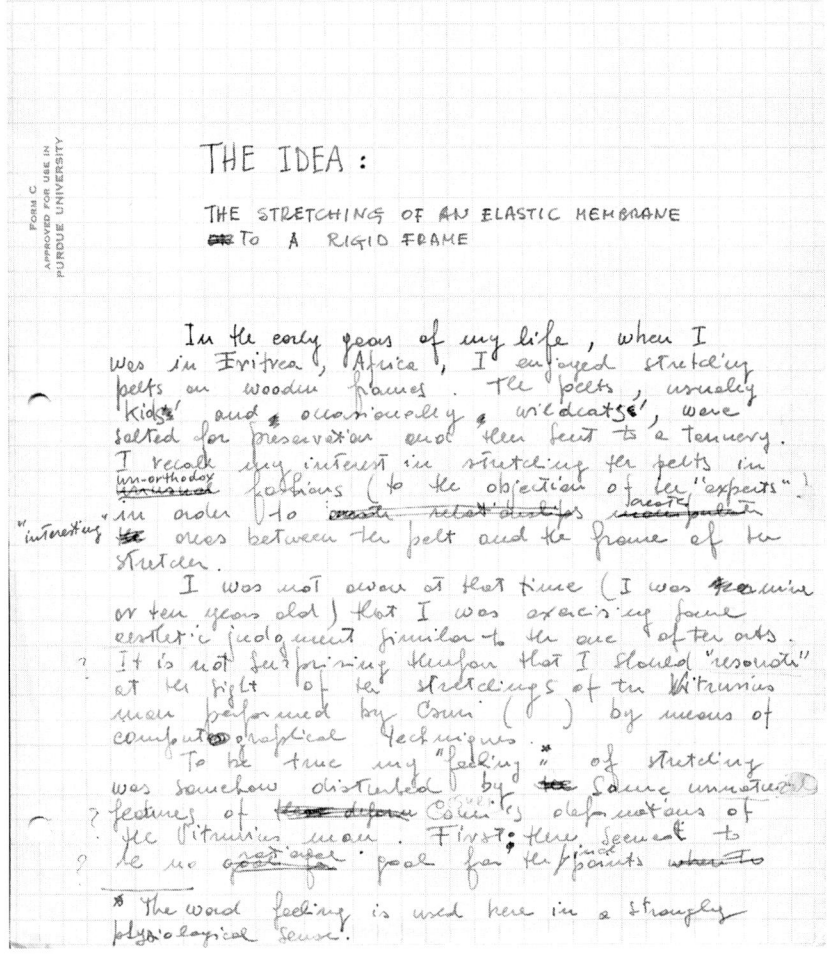

THE IDEA:

THE STRETCHING OF AN ELASTIC MEMBRANE
TO A RIGID FRAME

In the early years of my life, when I was in Eritrea, Africa, I enjoyed stretching pelts on wooden frames. The pelts, usually 'kids' and occasionally 'wildcats', were salted for preservation and then sent to a tannery. I recall my interest in stretching the pelts in un-orthodox fashions (to the objection of the "experts") in order to [crossed out] "interesting" areas between the pelt and the frame of the stretcher.

I was not aware at that time (I was eight, nine or ten years old) that I was exercising some aesthetic judgment similar to the one of the arts. It is not surprising therefore that I should "resonate" at the sight of the stretchings of the Vitruvian man performed by Csuri (?) by means of computer-graphical techniques.

To be true my "feeling" of stretching was somehow disturbed by two some unnatural features of the Csuri's deformations of the Vitruvian man. First: there seemed to be no rational pool for the points where to

* The word feeling is used here in a strongly physiological sense.

Figure 54. Original Stretch manuscript reproduced in this book.

of the membrane, the presence of holes, . . .) which in turn influences the deformations of the membrane.

One could resort to considering the "finite membrane" as part of an infinite membrane without cuts or holes. But even this simplification would not work. In fact, since to accomplish finite deformations one should apply finite forces at the pinching points, infinitely strong stresses would appear around the pinching points.

Besides this difficulties, the sheer amount of time required to integrate the partial differential equations in a two dimensional domain would be prohibitive.

Since the purpose of this inquiry is to be found at the illustrative or artistic level, the "solution" of the problem must be understood as not necessarily coincident with the mathematical solution of the physical problem of stretching a membrane. The result of the operation of stretching should be such that the eye, not the mathematical formulas, accept it as an actual stretch.

It was therefore resolved to formulate a mapping process that would simulate, from the visual viewpoint, the actual stretching of a membrane.

PUEBLO [1982]

PUEBLO by Aldo Giorgini, Mar. 82

- photographic rendition of a color image on the CRT
  screen of a Tektronix 4027 A
- camera: Nikkormat
- film: Kodachrome 64 (f4, 1sec.)
- paper: Kodak
        program used: PHOTO by Giorgini, Smith
        program used: PALZION by Aldo Giorgini

This work has had a controlled stochastic component during
its design phase. A regular noise sequence was superposed to the
planned signal sequence in the line from the host computer to the
color terminal.
What was supposed to be a Canyon representation turned out
to be a random pattern. The rendition presented here is the result
of several additional purposeful operations which rearranged some
elements of the original picture.
It should be ~~recognized~~ *considered* as a form of computer aided collage.
The lesson learned in the process of using the noise stream,
has led to another form of representation which is no longer a
collage, but a complete design, with a random element which is a
"built-in" feature of the program, to be used when the line is
noiseless.
An example of built-in controlled stochastic components
is given by CORTEN STEEL, presented in this show.

20 Prints Limited Edition($200, unframed)

Figure 55. *Pueblo* art statement.

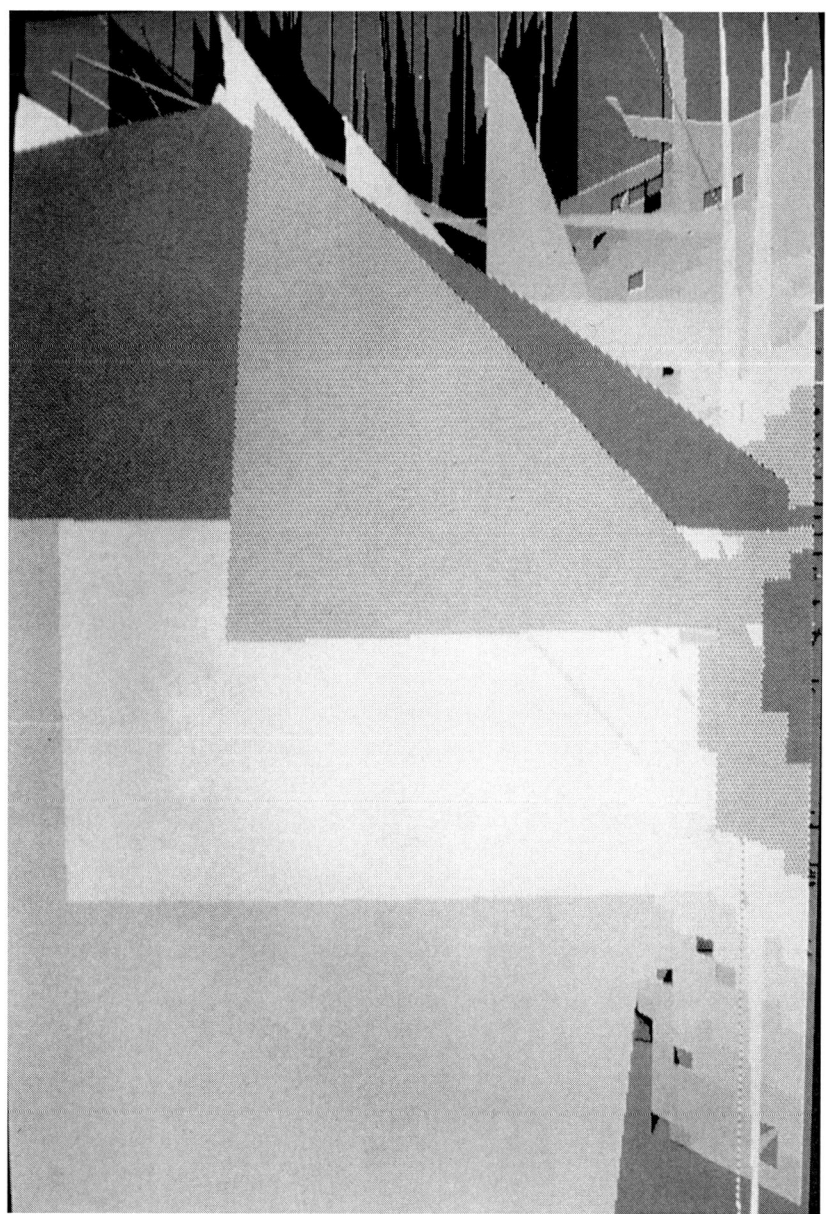

Figure 56. *Pueblo,* 1982. 35 mm Kodachrome slide.

Notes

1. [Giorgini's note] The adjective virtual is used here to denote the fact that the 64 colors of the palette cannot be used simultaneously.
2. Included in this book as Figure 36.
3. According to his 1984 CV, this technical report, numbered CE-HSE-81-3, was "in print." After documenting Giorgini's estate, I found no evidence that this article or report was ever printed. However, "Stretch" provided Giorgini with a framework for manipulating vector primitives using his own mathematical model. Although "Stretch" was listed as a technical report in 1981, Giorgini had a prior body of work in 1976 that demonstrated the use of stretching algorithms, like in the case of the *Surfaces* series. Alternating black-and-white patterns and stretching them was part of Giorgini's signature style. This document was a collaboration with graduate students Sina Tamaddon and Shahriar Ghaemmaghami. Originally from Iran, Tamaddon served as vice president of applications at Apple until recent years, and he is considered to be one of the successors of Steve Jobs, according to *CNN Money* in 2010.

V. A BIOGRAPHICAL SKETCH OF ALDO GIORGINI

ALDO GIORGINI BIOGRAPHICAL SKETCH

1934
Born in Voghera, Italy

1937
Family moves to Decamere, Eritrea

1944
Becomes Carlo Ingegneri's apprentice

1949
Returns to Voghera
Becomes Ambrogio Casati's apprentice

1952
Starts engineering undergraduate studies at the University of Pavia, Italy
Graduates as *dottore* of mechanical engineering at the Politecnico di Torino, Italy

1959
Becomes associate professor of hydraulics at the Politecnico di Torino, Italy
Fulbright scholar at Colorado State University in Fort Collins

1964
Marries Elena
Graduates with a PhD in civil engineering from Colorado State

1966
Postdoctoral fellow at the National Center for Atmospheric Research in Boulder, Colorado
Conducts first experiments in computational visualization

1967
Becomes assistant professor of civil engineering at Purdue University in West Lafayette, Indiana

1973
Solo show at the Washington Gallery in Frankfort, Indiana
Solo show at the Krannert Gallery at Purdue University

1974
Invites Robert Mallary to Purdue as an artist-in-residence
Develops the software Fields
Presents at a MACAA panel on Computer Art in DeKalb, Illinois

1975
Organizes the "Computer Art Day" symposium at Purdue
Develops the *Surfaces* portfolio

1976
Featured in *Artist and Computer* by Ruth Leavitt

1977

Installs computer art murals at the A. A. Potter Engineering Center at Purdue

1978

Death of Elena

1979

Develops the software Stretch
Develops the software Palette and Photo

1980

Art In/Art Out exhibit at the Ukrainian Institute of Modern Art in
  Chicago
Solves a boundary dispute between Indiana and Kentucky through
  computational simulation and visualization

1981

Grant from the Apple Education Foundation to develop Apple Hydraulics
Computer Art Exhibit and Festival at Lehigh University in Bethlehem,
  Pennsylvania

1982

The work *Corten Steel* is awarded by the German Computer Graphics
  and Computer Art Society

1986

Surfaces receives an honorable mention at the Indianapolis Museum of
  Art and also is included in the National Collection of Fine Arts of
  the Smithsonian in Washington, DC
Invited to scientific conferences in Japan and Morocco as a specialist on
  fluid visualization

1988

Spends free time designing punk rock albums and flyers

1994

Dies in Indianapolis due to brain cancer

REFERENCES

Baecker, Ron, and Lynn Smith. GENESYS: An Interactive Computer-Mediated Animation System. 16 mm film. 1970. MIT Lincoln Laboratory. http://www.youtube.com/watch?v=GYIPKLxoTcQ.

Berzowska, Joanna. Guest Editorial. *Leonardo: Journal of the International Society for the Arts, Sciences and Technology* 44, no. 4 (2011): 296–97. http://dx.doi.org/10.1162/LEON_e_00204.

Bullock, Larry. "CE Prof Giorgini Connects Art, Science." *Journal and Courier,* March 14, 1974. http://www.soniciguana.com/AldoEXP/CEProf.htm.

Castaños-Ales, Enrique. "Los Orígenes del Arte Cibernético en España." 2000. http://www.enriquecastanos.com/tesisindice.htm.

CE 340 students. "CE 340 students to Aldo Giorgini." 1993. From Giorgini Estate.

"Computer Art Day." *Journal and Courier*, March 22, 1975.

"'Computer Art Day' Scheduled for Purdue." *Exponent*, March 24, 1975.

"Computer Graphics #3." *A Quarterly Report of SIGGRAPH-ACM* 3, no. 3 (1969).

Cooper, Douglas. "Very Nervous System." *Wired Magazine,* March 1995.

Csuri, Charles. "Computer Animation." *SIGGRAPH '75 Proceedings of the 2nd annual Conference on Computer Graphics and Interactive Techniques* 9, no. 1 (1975): 92–101. http://dx.doi.org/10.1145/563732.563746.

Curnutte, Mark. "Club Plays High Energy Music: Spud Zero Fans are Receptive to New Sounds." *Journal and Courier*, April 15, 1988.

Davis, Douglas. "The Computer: Final Fusion." In *Art and the Future: A History/Prophecy of the Collaboration Between Science, Technology, and Art,* 96–105. New York: Praeger Publishers, 1973.

DeMaria, Jean Dominici. "A Study of the Work of Charles Csuri, Computer Artist and Computer Art Educator." PhD diss., New York University, 1991.

Garcia, Esteban. "Photo and Palette: Early Pixel-Based Computer Art." Paper presented at the Media Art Histories 2013: RENEW the 5th International Conference on the Histories of Media Art, Science, and Technology, Riga, Latvia, October 8–11, 2013.

Garcia, Esteban. "Stretch: An Early Software Art Framework by Aldo Giorgini." Paper presented at the 19th International Symposium of Electronic Arts, Sydney, Australia, June 7–16, 2013. http://www.isea2013.org/events/digital-experimental-arts/.

Garcia, Esteban, and David Whittinghill. "Art and Code: The Aesthetic Legacy of Aldo Giorgini." *Leonardo: Journal of the International Society for the Arts, Sciences, and Technology* 44, no. 4 (2011): 309–16.

Gardner, William. "Interactive Display Techniques for the Tektronix 4027 Colour Terminal." *Displays* 2, no. 1 (1980): 45–55. http://dx.doi.org/10.1016/0141-9382(80)90194-8.

Giorgini, Aldo. *Aesthetics in Technology.* 1975. From Giorgini estate.

Giorgini, Aldo. "Aldo Giorgini." In *Artist and Computer*, edited by Ruth Leavitt, 9–12. New York: Creative Computing Press, 1976.

Giorgini, Aldo. *Apple Hydraulics.* 1983. From Giorgini estate.

Giorgini, Aldo. *Artist Statements.* 1982. From Giorgini estate.

Giorgini, Aldo. "Bridges as Sculptures?" Paper presented at the American Society of Civil Engineers, Atlanta, GA, 1979.

Giorgini, Aldo. *Palette: A Color Mixture System for Tektronix 4027.* 1980. From Giorgini estate.

Giorgini, Aldo. *Photo: Computer Code.* 1982. From Giorgini estate.

Giorgini, Aldo, Andrea Rinaldo, H. R. Lemmer, and A. R. Rao. "Graphec: A Graphic Laboratory for HEC2." Paper presented at the American Society of Civil Engineers, Las Vegas, NV, 1982. From Giorgini estate.

Giorgini, Aldo, Dean Randall, and Andrea Rinaldo. "The Indiana-Kentucky Boundary Dispute: An Unorthodox Approach to River Hydraulics." *Proceedings of the Indiana Academy of Science*, USA, 1981.

Giorgini, Aldo, and Wei-Chung Chen. "Interfaces, Computer Aided Art: The Program 'FIELDS.'" West Lafayette, IN: Purdue University, 1975.

Giorgini, Massimiliano. "Aldo Giorgini: 1934–1994." From Giorgini estate.

Hertlein, Grace. "Computer Art for Computer People: A Syllabus" *SIGGRAPH '77 Proceedings of the 4th annual Conference on Computer Graphics and Interactive Techniques* 9, no. 1 (1977): 249–54. http://dx.doi.org/10.1145/563858.563902.

Jankel, Annabel, and Rocky Morton. *Creative Computer Graphics.* New York: Cambridge University Press, 1984.

Jungers, Al. *Al Jungers to Aldo Giorgini.* January 28, 1988. From Giorgini Estate.

Kurzweil, Raymond. *The Age of Intelligent Machines.* Cambridge, MA: MIT Press, 1990.

Lambert, Nicholas. "A Critical Examination of 'Computer Art.'" Master's thesis, Oxford University, 2007. http://test.lambertsblog.co.uk/wp-content/uploads/2008/02/some-questions-about-computer-art-from-nick-lamberts-thesis.pdf.

Leavitt, Ruth, ed. *Artist and Computer.* New York: Creative Computing Press, 1976.

Lipsky, Jackie. "Jackie Lipsky to Aldo Giorgini." February 27, 1984. From Giorgini Estate.

Mallary, Robert. *Computer Art/Purdue.* Audiocassette. 1975.

Noll, Michael. "The Beginnings of Computer Art in the United States: A Memoir." *Leonardo: Journal of the International Society for the Arts, Sciences and Technology* 27, no. 1 (1994): 39–44.

Oster, Gerald. "Moiré Patterns and Visual Hallucinations." *Psychedelic Review* 7 (1966): 33–40.

Price, Lois. "Line, Shade & Shadow: Fabrication and Preservation of Architectural Drawings." Paper presented at Brodsky Series for the Advancement of Architectural Drawings, Syracuse University, October 2011. http://surface.syr.edu/pres_brodsky/7.

Purdue University Computing Center (PUCC). "Statement of Usage Charges." 1984. From Giorgini estate.

Reardon, Christopher. "Purdue Prof Helped Solve River Fight." *Journal and Courier*, October 21, 1981.

Ritzenthaler, Mary. "Creating a Preservation Environment." In *Preserving Archives and Manuscripts*, 109–51. Chicago: The Society of American Archivists, 2010.

Rosen, Margit, ed. *A Little-Known Story About a Movement, a Magazine, and the Computer's Arrival in Art: New Tendencies and Bit International, 1961–1973.* Cambridge, MA: MIT Press, 2011.

Shoup, Richard. "SuperPaint: An Early Frame Buffer Graphics System." *IEEE Annals of the History of Computing* 23, no. 2 (2001): 32–37. http://dx.doi.org/10.1109/85.929909.

Smith, Roberta. "Robert Mallary, 69, Junk Artist Behind the Growth of Sculpture." *New York Times*, February 15, 1997. http://www.nytimes.com/1997/02/15/arts/robert-mallary-69-junk-artist-behind-the-growth-of-sculpture.html.

Travis, J. R., and Aldo Giorgini. *Numerical Simulation of the Navier-Stokes Equations in Fourier Space.* Lafayette, IN: Hydromechanics Laboratory, Purdue University, 1975.

van Dam, Andries. "Computer Graphics Comes of Age: An Interview with Andries van Dam." *Communications of the ACM* 27, no. 7 (1984): 638–48. http://dx.doi.org/10.1145/358105.358190.

Walton, Lloyd B. "Aldo the Artist, Former Computer Scientist." *Indianapolis Star Magazine*, May 8, 1977.

Wiener, Norbert. *Cybernetics: Or the Control and Communication in the Animal and the Machine.* Cambridge, MA: MIT Press, 1948.

INDEX